The Listening Composer

DENSITY 21.5*

Flute Solo

EDGARD VARÈSE

* Written in January, 1936, at the request of Georges Barrère for the inauguration of his platinum flute. Revised April, 1946. 21.5 is the density of platinum.

** Always strictly in time—follow metronomic indications.

*** Notes marked + to be played softly, hitting the keys at the same time to produce a percussive effect.

Varèse, *Density 21.5*

The Ernest Bloch Professorship of Music and
the Ernest Bloch Lectures were established at the
University of California in 1962 to bring distinguished
figures in music to the Berkeley campus from time to
time. Made possible by the Jacob and Rosa Stern
Musical Fund, the professorship was founded in
memory of Ernest Bloch (1880–1959), Professor of
Music at Berkeley from 1940 to 1959.

GEORGE PERLE

The Listening Composer

UNIVERSITY OF CALIFORNIA PRESS

BERKELEY / LOS ANGELES / OXFORD

University of California Press
Berkeley and Los Angeles, California

University of California Press, Ltd.
Oxford, England

© 1990 by
The Regents of the University of California

Library of Congress Cataloging-in-Publication Data

Perle, George, 1915–
   The listening composer / George Perle.
      p.   cm. — (The Ernest Bloch lectures)
   ISBN 0-520-06991-9 (alk. paper)
    1. Perle, George, 1915–   —Criticism and interpretation.
  2. Music—20th century—History and criticism.   I. Title.
  II. Series.
  ML410.P2925A3   1990
  780′.92—dc20   89-20436
                                             CIP
                                             MN

Printed in the United States of America

1 2 3 4 5 6 7 8 9

The paper used in this publication meets the minimum requirements
of American National Standard for Information Sciences—Perma-
nence of Paper for Printed Library Materials, ANSI Z39.48-1984. ⊗™

FOR SHIRLEY

CONTENTS

The present volume consists of a series of six public lectures I delivered as Visiting Ernest Bloch Professor of Music at the University of California at Berkeley during the Spring 1989 semester, and of additional material on some of the same topics presented in a concurrent seminar.

It thus addresses a wide spectrum of readers, not all of whom will find that additional material accessible. But neither is the latter a prerequisite for an understanding of those other parts of this book in which the same concepts are approached in a different way and from a different direction. A substantiation of some of these concepts can only take the form of a theoretical treatise, but even those readers with the professional interests, education, and experience to make their way through my substantiation, in Lecture V, of the role of symmetry in the formation of a post-diatonic harmonic language should not feel obliged to do so before moving on to Lecture VI, some parts of which will certainly be accessible—and, I hope, of interest—to the general reader as well.

I am indebted to my friends and former pupils David Pitt and Elliott Antokoletz and, of course, to my wife, Shirley Rhoads, for their careful reading of the manuscript and for their many, and very valuable, suggestions.

Berkeley, California
May 8, 1989

LECTURE I   # Turning Screws and
Slicing Apples

Shortly after I was invited to assume the Ernest Bloch professorship I came upon an article by John Updike that made me even more uneasy than I would otherwise have been about the entailed responsibility in presenting a series of public lectures. I have never heard him but am informed, by people who have, that Mr. Updike is an excellent lecturer. Nevertheless, this is what he has to say, in the June 16, 1988, issue of the *New York Review of Books*, on the subject of creative writers as lecturers: "Asking a writer to lecture is like asking a knife to turn a screw. Screws are necessary to hold the world together, the tighter the better, and a screwdriver is an admirable tool, more rugged and versatile and less dangerous than a knife; but a knife with a broken tip and dulled or twisted edge serves all purposes poorly. Of course, if a knife is repeatedly used as a screwdriver, it will get worn into the shape of one; but then don't expect it to slice any more apples." I've been a college teacher for about forty years, so the role of lecturer is not unfamiliar to me, but whenever I've been called upon to address an audience on the subject of my own work as a composer I've had an uncomfortable sense of engaging in some inappropriate and awkward activity, like trying to turn a screw with a knife or to slice an apple with a screwdriver.

The subject of these lectures is of my own choosing. In what sense is that subject my own work, my own life as a composer?

A few years ago—1985, the Berg centenary, to be precise—I received a phone call from the producer of a television show, inviting me to give a talk on Alban Berg. I explained that I would not be able to accept, because of conflicts due to a pending concert of my own music. "But you're not the same George Perle who composes, are you?" said the voice at the other end of the line. But I am indeed the same George Perle, and especially so in connection with these talks, an alternative title for which might have been "Tradition in 20th Century Music." But given the plethora of totally opposed compositional styles, compositional techniques, and even compositional languages today, can one speak of "Tradition in 20th Century Music," and if so, what can one mean by it? I have interpreted the above quotation from John Updike as an admonition to lay my cards on the table right away and admit that I do not present a consensual view of my subject. My words come from my own perspective as a composer, a personal perspective formed by my own need to find a way to write music that would do what music has always done, that would be coherent in the way music has always been coherent, that would be new in its language and materials only to the extent that the realization of this aim in our time demands newness in its language and materials.

My second book, published in 1977, bears the same title as an article I published thirty-four years earlier, *Twelve-Tone Tonality*. The title alone is enough to suggest that, in spite of our common interest in tonality, my view of tradition is not the same as that of the sponsors of a recent competition for compositions "in any style which relies partially or wholly on any major/minor key systems or modes." Neither is my perspective the same as that of an article on current trends in contemporary composition which appeared in the magazine section of the *New York Times* a few years ago under the title "The New

Romance with Tonality." But if the qualification of "tonality" in my title deprives me of the advantages of a shared perspective, doesn't it also suggest a similar deprivation in my relation to the tradition of twelve-tone composition?

My own romance with tonality is an old one. It predates my 1943 article by more than two decades. In fact, when I fell in love with tonality for the first time Schoenberg had not even quite arrived at his concept of an ordered statement of the twelve pitch classes as a consistent basis for atonal composition, though he was on the verge of this discovery. The first piece I can recall hearing as a coherent, integrated musical experience was the Etude in F minor from the *Trois Nouvelles Etudes* of Chopin. My Russian immigrant father had bought a piano in anticipation of the arrival of his niece, a pianist, from the Old Country. I was six or seven at the time. The experience of hearing her play this piece was so intense, so startling, as to induce a traumatic change of consciousness. What could I have known about "tonality"? Yet I must have "understood" this music, I must have been able to "follow" it. And what is it that we "follow" in a piece of music, what is it that gives it coherence and direction and sense, if not, in the largest sense of that term, its "tonality"?

This same cousin was my first piano teacher. It was not a happy relationship. My own identification was with the source of that music, transcendent though it seemed. I knew right away that what I had to do as a musician was compose, but my teacher seemed to be surprised by this notion. She gave me the impression that this was no longer done, that everything had already been composed by people who were now dead. She was living with us at the time, and so, to our mutual distress, she was often within earshot when I was supposed to be practicing. She could not understand why my practice sessions would be interrupted by long periods of silence, and she complained to my mother about this. I remember one of these silent periods very well, because it was during this particular pause in my practicing that I had my second great musical experience, one that was very different from my first hearing of the Chopin etude—not at all transcendent and magical, as that had been, but equally decisive and compelling for its very difference. I noticed something remarkable about the simple, accompanied folksong I was practicing. Its two halves, each eight bars long, were exactly alike, except that the order of the two chords that concluded the first half was reversed at the conclusion of the second. I had discovered, all by myself, the difference between the half cadence and the full cadence. More than that, I had discovered the meaning of cadence in general. Most of all, I had discovered a connection between music and our normal life outside of music, for I saw an analogy between music and speech: the first half of the piece was something like a question, and the second half something like an answer. This was my first act of musical analysis and the beginning of my career as a theorist, but it was also the beginning of my career as a composer, for it was not until this moment that I saw music as something tangible, as something that could be "understood" in a different sense from the way I had "understood" the Chopin etude at that first hearing, as something that I, too, could learn to compose.

Both these ways of understanding were, of course, bound up with the traditional harmonic language of Western music. This meant that as my understanding of that language evolved, as my familiarity with its literature developed and as I labored to discover and to invent my own voice in it, I, too, found myself bound up with the ambiguities and contradictions that had led to a revolutionary transformation in that language in the music of Schoenberg and his circle a generation earlier. The crisis in my own development came in 1937, when I was twenty-two years old. It seemed to me that the musical language itself had become problematical. It no longer seemed possible to write music that was really significant, because the traditional means of harmonic progression and structure no longer worked, and while there were other ways to write music, they couldn't provide a basis for a really coherent, complex, and integrated musical language such as had been the basis of Western music for some three hundred years. The music of Debussy, Ravel, Stravinsky, Richard Strauss, Sibelius only seemed to confirm, in their different ways, the demise of the great tradition. There was a kind of indigenous American "atonal" tendency whose most successful representative was Carl Ruggles and to which my teacher, Wesley LaViolette, also belonged. Though this was hardly significant enough to call a "school" an attempt was being made to formulate certain principles for it under the rubric of "dissonant counterpoint."[1] I could find nothing in this to meet my own needs and was not at all inclined to forsake my own neo-classical idiom for it. Of Schoenberg's music I had heard only Stokowski's recording of *Gurrelieder* and, on a distant radio station and through a great deal of static, a live performance of the Second Quartet, and I had been powerfully impressed by both. Of Schoenberg's later works I knew nothing. The American premiere of *Wozzeck* in 1931 had created enough of a stir that, though I was only fifteen at the time and living on a farm in Indiana, news of it reached me and I eventually managed to borrow a score from the Chicago Public Library; but it was a bit too soon, and I could make nothing of it. By the time of Berg's death on Christmas Eve, 1935, the Second Vienna School was largely written off as having had its day. An obituary by one who was sympathetic to that circle began:

[1]Charles Seeger, "On Dissonant Counterpoint," *Modern Music* VII/4 (June–July 1930); Henry Cowell, *New Musical Resources* (1930; reprint ed., New York: Something Else Press, 1969), pp. 35–42.

With the untimely death of Alban Berg it would appear that the period of atonal composition is for the time being already concluded. The prospects for European music become, by this, still darker than they were already. The Schoenberg group had at its disposition no single individual who could take the place of Berg. . . . There is here in Europe no longer much prospect of progress, of recovery. German music is almost completely demobilised; France and Italy bring forward innocent little pieces and tame pasticcios; the music of the Russians fulfils, perhaps, cultural duties of significance, but it is, speaking from the point of view of musical history, continually pre-1914, to my thinking. The innovations of Arnold Schoenberg and his group threaten, together with the death of the greatest talent in this group, to become petrified; and that already now, within twenty-five years.[2]

If I was equally pessimistic about the state of contemporary music a year and a half later, it was only because I was not yet aware of "the innovations of Schoenberg and his group."

My first acquaintance with these innovations came through an accidental encounter, in the summer of 1937, with the score of Berg's *Lyric Suite*. The first page was enough to give me an insight into the nature of my difficulties. I saw at once that it was possible to comprehend the twelve notes of the semitonal scale as an integral and autonomous collection, that it was possible "to dissociate, so to speak, the chromatic scale from 'chromaticism,'"[3] and I suddenly understood that I had unconsciously been searching for such a possibility.

I was not instantly transformed by this experience into a composer of twelve-tone serial music. Of the post-diatonic "system" that

[2]Willem Pijper, *Musical Times* 77 (May 1936): 414.
[3]George Perle, *Serial Composition and Atonality: An Introduction to the Music of Schoenberg, Berg, and Webern* (Berkeley and Los Angeles: University of California Press, 1962; 5th ed., 1981), p.1.

Schoenberg was rumored to have devised I could not have known more at the time than what Henry Cowell had reported in his chapter on "dissonant counterpoint" in his speculative book *New Musical Resources*:

> Schönberg, though, has another quite different new system of counterpoint of his own which he has worked with consistency, which he employs with straightforward logic in his later works, and which is formulated so that he teaches the method to his students.
>
> . . . Schönberg in his system does not formulate new polyphonic materials, but takes from ancient counterpoint devices which had become almost obsolete, such as retrograde, inverse melodic line, etc., as well as better-known contrapuntal usages, and applies them to a twelve-tone scale in which each tone is independent. By an ingenious method of geometric diagram he is able to discover every possible variation of the themes and is therefore able to select the form of development which seems to him the most perfect.[4]

The obsessive analytical studies of the *Lyric Suite* that I undertook from the moment I played the opening bars at the piano were motivated in the first place by the extraordinary and immediate effect of this new and complex music. But I also hoped that they would give me some insight into Schoenberg's "new system of counterpoint" and into whatever it was that Cowell meant by his "ingenious method of geometric diagram." In this I was disappointed. Neither from the *Lyric Suite* nor from any other work of Berg's is it possible to deduce the basic premises of Schoenberg's twelve-tone system. The twelve-tone collection unfolded by the first three chords of the *Lyric Suite* is inconsistent with the twelve-tone series that commences in the sec-

[4]Cowell, *New Musical Resources*, p. 41.

ond bar, according to whatever principles of derivation we can discover in Schoenberg's serial compositions. Between these two independent—according to Schoenberg's system—twelve-tone sets a six-note chord is interposed, but where is the complementary six-note collection that would give us the "missing" six notes of the twelve-tone "aggregate"?[5] The implications, for the concept of twelve-tone harmony, of the accompaniment to the first thematic statement of the series, and the procedures by which that accompaniment is derived from the series, are diametrically opposed to Schoenberg's practice. At the bottom of the first page of the score there is a second thematic version of the series, derived through the cyclical permutation of the first version. Such a procedure is not necessarily inconsistent with the premises of Schoenberg's system, but it is something we do not find in his work. And accompanying a three-part canon on this cyclically permuted statement of the series we again find something that is inconsistent with these premises, a retrograde statement of the first three chords in the form of a straightforward linear statement of the cycle of fifths which can only be construed as a second series. So much for the first nine bars of the *Lyric Suite* as a means toward understanding Schoenberg's "new system of counterpoint"! But perhaps none of these discrepancies is so much at odds with Schoenberg's serialism as the twelve-tone aggregate which we come to at the conclusion of the exposition of the first movement, which is not derivable in that system from either of the two series (ex. 1.1).

Since the tonal coherence and musical sense of the movement were unmistakable to me, I assumed that the introductory chords, the thematic series and the harmonic elements derived from it, the cyclically permuted statements of the thematic series, the linear statement of

---

[5]This is Milton Babbitt's term for a collection of the twelve pitch classes.

EXAMPLE 1.1

the cycle of fifths, and the hexachordal scales of the concluding subject must all be higher-level manifestations of a deeper background
structure which still remained for me to discover. In making such an
assumption I had taken the first step in what Joseph Kerman, in his
friendly comments on *Twelve-Tone Tonality*, calls a "private reading
of serialism."[6] But that private reading, as Professor Kerman points
out, is "emblematic of [my] traditional orientation." And a tradition,
of course, is not private. Neither can one really lay claim to a purely
personal perspective on a "tradition." If a tradition is not shared, it is
not a tradition. I might even say that the real subject of these lectures
is an explanation of the ways in which my "reading of serialism" is
not exclusively "private," of the ways in which my perspective is not
merely personal.

The alternative title that I have proposed for these lectures, "Tradition in 20th Century Music," implies that this tradition is a departure from an earlier tradition. But if we are really to understand the
respects in which this tradition is new, we have also to understand in
what respects it is not different from the tradition that precedes it.

In every edition of Schoenberg's Opus 11 that precedes the *Gesamtausgabe* we find the same notational discrepancy in the tenth bar from
the end of the first movement (ex. 1.2). On the second beat of this
bar the note on the third space of the upper staff is preceded by a sharp
sign on the third line. Either the note or the sharp sign is misplaced,

[6]Joseph Kerman, *Contemplating Music* (Cambridge, Mass.: Harvard University
Press, 1985), p. 93.

EXAMPLE 1.2   Schoenberg, Op. 11, No. 1

Copyright 1910 by Universal Edition. Renewed Copyright 1938 by Arnold Schoenberg. Used by permission of Belmont Music Publishers.

but which is it? In my analysis of this piece in *Serial Composition and Atonality* I attribute a special role to the augmented triad, which not only "emerges . . . as the primary structural detail of a large part of the development section," but which also determines, through Schoenberg's ingenious large-scale exploitation of its special property—invariance of pitch-class content at three pitch levels—the overall tonal structure of the movement.[7] If we resolve the notational discrepancy in Example 1.2 by shifting the problematical note to the third line of the staff, "all four 'augmented triads' appear in sequence in this and the following bar, to confirm and clarify, at a strategic moment in the formal design, the harmonic basis of the composition."[8] Edward T. Cone proposes a different reason for resolving the notational discrepancy in the same way. Taking issue with the "correction" given in the *Gesamtausgabe*, which resolves the discrepancy by shifting the sharp sign to the third space, he writes:

Misguidedly, I had looked forward in the present publication to a confirmation of *b♯* which creates an augmented triad that sounds to me much more idiomatic here than the minor triad formed by the apparently correct *c♯*; even the major-minor clash produced by

[7]Perle, *Serial Composition and Atonality*, pp. 14f.
[8]Ibid., p. ix.

the latter seems insufficiently dissonant, within the vocabulary of this piece, to support the crescendo that it must. Hence I am inclined to mistrust the accepted solution, even if it turns out to have the authority of the manuscript behind it. The misprint might have arisen as a result of a correction or a revision made by the composer at some stage of proofreading, but incompletely adopted by the engraver or the printer.[9]

My reason for preferring *b♯* to *c♯* derives from revolutionary structural principles that mark Opus 11, No. 1 as a signal work of a new musical language. Professor Cone's argument is based on a principle of musical rhetoric that is as relevant to Beethoven and Wagner as it is to the new music of Schoenberg—that an increase in dynamic intensity will seem incongruous if it is joined to a concomitant decrease in harmonic tension.[10]

A striking example of the way in which dynamic changes can point up and clarify the meaning of structurally significant harmonic details is found in the opening bars of Varèse's *Density 21.5* (see frontispiece and endpapers). In the first five bars the tritone *c♯-g* unmistakably emerges as the boundary interval, and the midpoint of that interval, *e*, as unmistakably functions as a pivotal note, dividing the tritone into two minor thirds, functionally differentiated by the filling in of *e-g*, but not *c♯-e*, by a passing note. A continuation of that passing-

---

[9]Ibid., pp. ix f., quoted from Edward T. Cone, "Editorial Responsibility and Schoenberg's Troublesome 'Misprints,'" *Perspectives of New Music* XI/1 (Fall–Winter 1972).

[10]A composer may, of course, purposefully suppress an expected *crescendo* for the sake of the special effect of the suppression itself, as Beethoven does in the transition to the Finale of the Fifth Symphony, in the sixteen bars of increasing harmonic and melodic tension which culminate in the two sustained chords that complete the progression from C minor to C major. The frustrated *crescendo* is all the more powerful in its effect when it is finally released only upon the attainment of the climactic closing bars of the passage and when the dynamic energy that should have been given twenty-three bars to realize its potential is constrained to do so in a mere eight.

EXAMPLE 1.3

note motion in the three bars that follow gradually extends the upper limit of the boundary interval until closure is achieved in the arrival of the octave, on the downbeat of bar 9 (ex. 1.3). If I describe the octave, *c#-db* as something "achieved," it is because the composer himself describes it in this way, through the simultaneous attainment of a new dynamic level, *fortissimo*, and through the *Luftpause* which separates it from the preceding passing note—really a leading tone within the new context established by the octave as a boundary interval.

But if the attainment of closure, through the octave, is an "achievement," it is one that creates a crisis for the composer, as we can hear in his *subito* substitution of *mf* for the *fff* to which the *crescendo* sign seems to point in bar 9, and in his seeming inability, through two whole bars, to move beyond *db* and *c*, the point of closure and its leading tone. His partitioning of the octave in the first ten bars places Varèse with Scriabin and the Schoenberg circle among the revolutionary composers whose work initiates the beginning of a new mainstream tradition in the music of our century. Varèse's octave is symmetrically partitioned by the tritone, *c#-g* and *g-db*, instead of asymmetrically by the fifth degree of the diatonic scale into a perfect fifth and perfect fourth. The minor third, in turn, symmetrically partitions each statement of the tritone. The result is a closed cyclic system, the diminished-7th chord, which provides no internal basis for transposition or conversion. Having closed the minor-3rd cycle upon achieving the octave, the composer finds himself with no means of modulation or transition to another minor-3rd cycle or to some other type of harmonic structure. He can continue his composition only by wilfully breaking the symmetry that determines pitch relations in the first ten bars. That wilful break occurs in the sudden *crescendo* to *fff* which brings us to a new note, *d*, on the downbeat of bar 11. The dynamic markings tell us that both the arrival of the octave in bar 9 and the change to a new harmonic area in bar 11 come as something of a surprise to the composer himself, or so he would have us believe. A very different message would have been conveyed if these crucial moments in the unfolding of the movement had been presented as they are in my revised version in Example 1.4.

EXAMPLE 1.4

The harmonic language of this music would have seemed strange to Beethoven, but I think he might well have discovered a key to that language, though perhaps only after several hearings, in Varèse's structural use of dynamics, which is so much like his own. The second movement of the Fifth Symphony offers a striking illustration of this affinity in the sudden *fortissimo* on the German 6th chord in the seventh bar of the second theme, which takes us from the tonic key, A♭ major, to C major. Here is Tovey on the beginning of this movement:

> In form the movement is unique, if dimly suggested by Haydn's special form of variations on two alternating themes. But here the themes are of quite peculiar types. Violas and cellos . . . state the first theme in a single broad phrase, the end of which the higher instruments echo and carry on into a series of echoing after-

thoughts. Then the second theme begins, very simply, pauses on a wistful note, and suddenly bursts into a blaze of triumph in a remote key, C major, the tonic of the whole symphony.[11]

Why the sudden "blaze of triumph"? Through the change of key Beethoven makes his way out of a compositional impasse, just as Varèse had done by his introduction of a new pitch class outside the closed field of pitch relations on which the harmonic sense of everything up to that point had depended. But where Varèse simply cuts the Gordian knot, Beethoven's "triumph" is a brilliant intellectual achievement, drawing wonderfully subtle yet wonderfully logical inferences from the first theme of the movement. The "echoing afterthoughts" extend the first theme by reiterating the V-I cadence of the first eight bars through fourteen additional bars. The second theme (ex. 1.5) commences with two more statements of V-I in A♭, and it is then (bar 27) that it "pauses," on a *pianissimo* diminished-7th chord that introduces what I hear as a questioning rather than a "wistful" note. After so many "echoing afterthoughts" of the A♭ major cadence, should not the second theme be in another key? An affirmative answer, *fortissimo*, comes with an enharmonic addition of *f♯* to the A♭ major triad, converting it into a German 6th chord that resolves to a V-I cadence in the new key. With the first entrance, in C major, of horns and trumpets, the second theme "bursts into a blaze of triumph," but both the triumphant new motive in the new key and the progression from A♭ to C had been quietly presaged in the antecedent phrase of the first theme (ex. 1.6).[12]

---

[11]Donald Francis Tovey, *Essays in Musical Analysis* (London: Oxford University Press, 1935), vol. 1, p. 41.

[12]There is a striking interrelation of dynamics with harmony and formal design throughout the presentation of the two themes. In Example 1.6, for instance, everything is marked *piano* except for the *forte* on the penultimate bar. It is this which calls forth the "series of echoing afterthoughts."

EXAMPLE 1.5   Beethoven, Symphony No. 5, 2nd mvt.

Viola

Cello

Bass

EXAMPLE 1.6

EXAMPLE 1.7

I referred a moment ago to the revolutionary implications of Varèse's symmetrical partitioning of the octave in *Density 21.5*, as opposed to the asymmetrical partitioning that characterizes the octave in diatonic music. Let us suppose that we are hearing this work for the first time. At what point would we recognize it as an "atonal" rather than a tonal composition? Suppose the composer had completed the first phrase by descending from *g* to *f♯* (ex. 1.7)? I think this would have led us to hear the G as a dissonant upper neighbor resolving to the dominant. Having taken us as far as I show in Example 1.3, does the composer still have the option of subsequently employing a progression such as I show in Example 1.7, or does Example 1.3 establish a context that would be inconsistent with such a progression? Is the *f♯* that I have appended to the first phrase of *Density 21.5* analogous in its implications to the chord that I have appended to the first phrase of the *Tristan* Prelude in Example 1.8? Not at all, because, in fact, this phrase does eventually resolve to the tonic triad, though in a long-range and extraordinary way, and with the major form of the triad substituted for the minor. The difference be-

EXAMPLE 1.8

EXAMPLE 1.9

EXAMPLE 1.10

tween what Wagner does here and what some other composer might
have done is a stylistic one. In the context of Wagner's musical language the V–I cadence still retains its relevance. But the concept of
the perfect fourth or fifth as a referential interval relative to which the
tritone requires resolution, as implied in Example 1.7, has no relevance at all to *Density 21.5*.

Here is the beginning of another famous opening phrase, closer in
character to the Varèse in that it too is for solo flute and prominently
features the interval of a tritone (ex. 1.9). Suppose we continue as
shown in Example 1.10, interpreting the tritone, *c#-g*, as a dissonant
interval and resolving it into the minor third, *g#-b*. In fact, what Example 1.10 shows is Debussy's own continuation of the first two bars,
except that he paraphrases this conventional resolution of the disso-

EXAMPLE 1.11

EXAMPLE 1.12

nant tritone by displacing *g♯* to the upper octave (ex. 1.11), thus en-
larging the ambitus to a new and more strongly dissonant interval,
the octave plus a semitone, and at the same time providing space for
the unfolding of the complete E major triad.

But, before we get to this displaced resolution, the repetition of the
tritone and the whole-tone ascent from *g* suggest a step in the direction of the Varèse composition, i.e., in the direction of a symmetrical
rather than the conventional tonal interpretation of the tritone.[13]
Would we have been surprised if Debussy had continued to the octave
of the lower *g*, as in Example 1.12? You may prefer Debussy's own
version of the opening bars of *L'Après-midi d'un faune* to the one I have
just proposed, but this should not lead you to draw any conclusions about the respective merits of the different harmonic worlds
represented in the two examples. I'm sure you found my tonal version of the opening of *Density 21.5* equally uninteresting in comparison to the original.

Example 1.12 immediately puts us in the harmonic world of *Den-*

---

[13]Perhaps it is because of this whole-tone ascent that Debussy spells the lowest note
as *g* instead of as the *f×* that the key would imply.

EXAMPLE 1.13

sity 21.5—and of *Le Sacre* as well. The tritone boundary of the principal theme of the Introduction to *Le Sacre* (ex. 1.13) plays the same structural role for Stravinsky as it does for Varèse in *Density 21.5*. It symmetrically partitions the octave and is itself symmetrically partitioned into two minor thirds. (I will explain later why I regard this, rather than that fragment of a Lithuanian folksong we have all come to know so well, as the principal theme of the Introduction.)

As Leverkühn's Devil in Thomas Mann's *Dr. Faustus* tells us, "Composing itself has got too hard, devilishly hard." The very act of composing today raises questions, or should raise questions, that at one time did not need to be asked. Professor Cone finds a passage in Schoenberg's Opus 11 as given in the *Gesamtausgabe* "insufficiently dissonant . . . to support the crescendo." What determines "sufficiency" of dissonance in the harmonic language of Opus 11, and how, indeed, do we define "dissonance" in that language? We have seen how dynamic relations play the same structural role in an atonal composition by Varèse that they play in a tonal composition by Beethoven. What other elements in the practice of those composers whom Tovey regarded as *The Main Stream of Music* remain similarly relevant to those whom I would regard as the main stream of twentieth-century music? When we substituted, in Example 1.12, the octave of the lower *g* natural for Debussy's octave-displaced *g♯*, we eliminated the function of the latter as a note of resolution, and thereby the special effect of the octave displacement as well. What meaning can octave displacement have in general for atonal or twelve-tone music? I propose to put this question in another way: when are the twelve elements of the tone row "pitches" and when are they "pitch classes"?[14]

Registral displacement and the determination of dynamic values are concerns that are directly relevant to the act of composition. We have so far overlooked other, implicit, questions that are of a more restrictedly theoretical character. When Professor Cone refers to degrees of "dissonance" in Schoenberg's Opus 11 he is reverting to the layman's use of that term, which has to do with the relative "harshness" of a collection of pitches, a quality that I tried to define more explicitly in my first book:

> Each of the different intervals has its own sonic quality or what has been called, for lack of a better term, "degree of tension." In isolation from any compositional context one can evaluate the "degree of tension" of the intervals from the "minor second" to the tritone as varying inversely with the size of the interval, and of those from the tritone to the "major seventh" . . . as varying directly with the size of the interval.[15]

In reference to music in the major/minor system, however, "dissonance" has only to do with the harmonic function of a collection of pitches. In tonal theory, any collection of pitches that is not a major or minor triad or a component of a major or minor triad is a "dissonance," and requires resolution to a "consonance." Since we have no accepted terminology for describing the relative "degree of tension" of a collection of pitches in post-tonal music—a highly ambiguous concept in any case—Professor Cone is quite right to borrow a

[14]We are, of course, indebted to Milton Babbitt for this useful and necessary term, which is defined as follows in the *New Grove*: "The set of all pitches that are transpositions of some given pitch by zero or an integral number of octaves. All *d*s, for example, are members of the pitch class *d*."

[15]Perle, *Serial Composition and Atonality*, pp. 30f.

non-professional usage that he would never employ under other circumstances and that we can all understand. I have described Varèse's *Density 21.5* as a post-tonal work in which the octave is symmetrically partitioned into a diminished-7th chord, and Schoenberg's Opus 11, No. 1 as a work in which another symmetrical structure, "the augmented triad, . . . determines . . . the overall tonal structure of the movement." In the traditional tonal theory from which we borrow this nomenclature for the two chord-types their names have very explicit implications that have no relevance whatever to post-tonal music. Both of them, like the twelve-tone scale itself, are cyclic structures, which is to say that each of them unfolds a single recurrent interval in a series that closes with a return to the initial pitch class. These interval cycles play a fundamental role in the harmonic organization of post-diatonic music and can easily be identified simply by naming the cycle.[16] Professor Cone's reference to a "major-minor clash" is more problematical, since it could lead one to conjecture that the pitch collection to which he thus refers is a particular chord-type with special characteristics that derive from the fact that it can be dissected into these familiar harmonic structures of traditional tonality.

At the beginning of this lecture I distinguished between two kinds of musical "understanding," one of which I inferred from my earliest recollected musical experience, my intuitive and spontaneous re-

---

[16]I have proposed a nomenclature in which the letter "C" followed by an interval-class number (0 through 6) designates the cycle. For example, the "diminished-7th chord" in *Density 21.5* is "C3"; the "augmented triad" in Opus 11, No. 1 is "C4." Since transpositions of any given interval cycle are mutually exclusive as to pitch-class content, we can identify the specific pitch-class collection by any one of its component pitch classes. I identify these by the integers 0 through 11, with 0 for pitch class *c*, 1 for *c#*, 2 for *d*, etc., and the specific transposition by employing as a subscript the lowest pitch-class number represented in the cycle. The first ten bars of *Density 21.5*, for example, are based on $C3_1$. (See George Perle, *The Operas of Alban Berg*. Vol. 2: *Lulu* [Berkeley and Los Angeles: University of California Press, 1985], pp. 199f.)

sponse to my first hearing of a Chopin etude, and the second of which
I inferred from my first act of musical analysis, my discovery of pe-
riodic structure in music through my recognition of the difference
between a half cadence and a full cadence. But in another sense of the
word I must *already* have "recognized" the difference between a half
cadence and a full cadence at that first hearing of the Chopin etude.
Otherwise this music would have been utterly incomprehensible to
me. And without this prior recognition there would have been nothing for me to analyze. Both kinds of understanding are bound up
with the compositional process. I cannot imagine Varèse working his
way to the octave in the first nine bars of *Density 21.5* through an
unfolding only of pitch and rhythmic relations, and then soberly
scrutinizing these nine bars in order to determine what kind of dynamic values might be appropriate to go with the notes. I think the
listening experience is extraordinarily complex, spontaneous, intuitive, naïve, and sophisticated, all at the same time, and that the composer already participates in the listening experience in the process of
composing. And I believe that the component of naïveté is at least as
essential a part of it as any of the others. Here is what the Nobel laureate Sir Peter Medawar has to say about creativity in science:

> Observation is the generative act in scientific discovery. For all its
> aberrations, the evidence of the senses is essentially to be relied
> upon—provided we observe nature as a child does, without prej-
> udices and preconceptions, but with that clear and candid vision
> which adults lose and scientists must strive to regain.[17]

"Clear and candid" listening is the "generative act" in composition.
In my analysis of the first nine bars of *Density 21.5* I explained why
Varèse marked his arrival at the octave with a *Luftpause* and a *fortis-*

[17]Peter Medawar, *Pluto's Republic* (Oxford: Oxford University Press, 1982),
p. 99.

simo, but I think it's quite possible that when he was composing these nine bars Varèse didn't "know" why, and didn't stop to find out. He simply "heard" it this way, and now the performer must "hear" it this way—it isn't enough for him to perform it this way merely because he sees the composer's "expression" markings on the printed page; if he's to get them right he must "hear" that what they mark is the arrival of the octave—and, eventually, so will the listener, or, at least, those listeners who really listen. And yet none of them may "know" why, in the way that I, and now you, too, know why.

Does this mean that a composer doesn't need the other kind of understanding of the difference between a half cadence and a full cadence? On the contrary, I find the notion of a composer who is not also a theorist incomprehensible, by which I do not mean that he has to write articles for, or even read, *Perspectives of New Music* or *The Journal of Music Theory*. The two kinds of musical understanding are directly, not inversely, related. They are related, one might say, in the way the area of a circle is related to its circumference. If we take what is inside the circle as a measure of the composer's conscious knowledge we can take its circumference as a measure of his intuitive knowledge, a measure of what impinges on whatever is outside the circle.

In addressing all these questions from my own viewpoint as a composer, I am speaking, I believe, for other composers, too—at least some other composers. Obviously, I am not speaking for a young composer, recently interviewed in the *New York Times*, "who began his composing career as a Serialist," then went on to "electronic and chance works," and eventually came to a "style [which] brought him to prominence a decade ago [that] involves Minimalist compositional techniques and rock instrumentation." Though I have no expectation that my work will ever achieve the kind of acceptance that this "musical pilgrim," as the *New York Times* calls him, found in his "progress" from "Serialism" to rock, the critics have often commented on the relative "accessibility" of my music compared to that of some other contemporary composers, and they have attributed this to a certain "humanity" in my attitude to the listener, a certain benevolence which leads me, as one critic has put it, to "meet the listener half-way." The fact is that when I compose I never think of and never have thought of meeting the listener. Or to put it another way that is more consistent with what I have just been saying about the process of composition, I'm the only listener with whom I'm concerned when I compose. Much as I appreciate the good opinion of music critics, I have to disclaim the suggestion that I am more "humane" than other composers.

Though no one has ever suggested that Anton Webern tried to "meet the listener half-way," and though the music I write is very different from his, my sense of what I am doing when I compose is very close to what his seems to have been:

> In one of his last letters to Hildegarde Jone, Webern describes the row of [a] projected cantata: "The last 3 notes are the 'retrograde' of the preceding ones, a condition that also obtains in the first half of the series. 'Motivically,' too, these 6 notes are the product of an arrangement that is *very strictly controlled* from several points of view: so they stand there on a foundation of *laws*!" For Webern composition was research into the "foundation of laws" that governs tone relations, and since both tone and man are part of nature it was research into—and here Webern quotes from Goethe—"the laws according to which nature in general, in the particular form of human nature, tends to produce and does produce when she can. . . ." Composing is not an "aesthetic" activity, but something analogous to the investigations of the "researcher into nature [who] strives to discover the rules of order that are the basis of nature."

A keynote of Webern's lectures on the new music was the aphorism "music is natural law as related to the sense of hearing," which he adapted from Goethe's "Color is natural law as related to the sense of sight." In one of the last letters to Reich, he writes: "Imagine the effect on me when I found this passage in [Hölderlin's] notes on the translation of Oedipus: 'Again, other works lack *infallibility*, compared with those of the Greeks; at least until now they've been judged by the impressions they make, rather than by their *ordered calculus* and all the other procedures *by which beauty is produced*.' Need I even say why I was so struck by the passage?" Elsewhere he quotes Goethe on the art of antiquity: "These high works of art were at the same time brought forth as humanity's highest works of nature, according to true and natural laws. Everything arbitrary or illusory falls away; here is necessity, here is God." "If only I could at last be understood a little!" he writes to Reich, referring to plans for an ISCM concert in Basel at which a number of his early pieces, then already thirty years old, were to be played. But in the end what have performances and an understanding audience to do with research into the "rules of order that are the basis of nature"?[18]

[18]George Perle, "Webern's Twelve-Tone Sketches," *Musical Quarterly* LVII/1 (January 1971): 24f. The following footnote to the above paragraph is quoted from this article: "Except for the excerpt from the letter to Jone [Webern, *Letters to Hildegarde Jone and Josef Humplik* (Bryn Mawr: Theodore Presser Company, 1967), pp. 17f.], all of the above quotations are taken from [Webern, *The Path to the New Music* (Bryn Mawr: Theodore Presser Company, 1963)]. Where Webern, in the informal lectures contained in this volume, tries to explain the 'natural laws' that govern sound and the relation of these 'laws' to the art of music, he shows himself to be as uninformed, naive, and inconsistent as most other composers, but this is beside the point. What is relevant is Webern's conception of the creative process as an expression of 'natural laws.'"

LECTURE II The Martian Musicologists

Richard Taruskin has speculated on what Martian musicologists might make of a pitch-class set analysis of the *Eroica Symphony*. He assumes that "they would not know that [the *Eroica*] is 'tonal,'" and that for them, therefore, pitch-class set analysis "would suffice."[1] I am not aware of a pitch-class set analysis of the *Eroica*, but I can point to other evidence that strongly suggests that we may, indeed, already have been invaded by "a troop of Martian musicologists."

Among the gratis desk copies of textbooks, student workbooks, anthologies, and other teaching aids that have come my way during a long teaching career, there is a demonstration tape for an electronic instrument that is supposed to make some of the most intricate contrapuntal techniques in the history of Western art music instantly available at the flick of a switch. The ignorance of tonality that Professor Taruskin imputes to the Martians is obviously shared by the inventor of the "Digionic Synthesizer." Otherwise he would have realized that in turning a Bach Invention upside down or backwards he deprives it of its tonal sense and makes it totally incoherent to us humans. But that is not enough to explain the failure of his project, which has had no perceptible influence on the practice or teaching of

[1] Richard Taruskin, "Reply to van den Toorn," *In Theory Only* 10/3 (October 1987): 56.

EXAMPLE 2.1

music. Thirty years earlier another apparently extraterrestrial musi-cologist who was equally unaware of the tonal character of the Bach Inventions had, for a time, an extraordinary impact on musical ped-agogy both within and beyond the academic community. That was before the age of computers and synthesizers, so Joseph Schillinger was under the same handicap, when he wanted to turn one of Bach's Inventions upside down or backwards, as Bach himself had been in composing the original version. He, too, as the inventor of the "Digionic Synthesizer" puts it, had to "waste time" writing it down. Perhaps this explains why, in his examples, Schillinger applies his "method of geometrical inversion" only to a single voice.[2] His ex-pectation, nevertheless, is that "by comparing the music of J. S. Bach . . . , the full range of what he could have done by using the method of geometrical inversions becomes clear." His example (ex. 2.1)

[2]Joseph Schillinger, *The Schillinger System of Musical Composition*, ed. L. Dowling and A. Shaw (1941; reprint ed., New York: Da Capo Press, 1976), pp. 193f.

EXAMPLE 2.2

EXAMPLE 2.3

shows the theme in its original version, backwards, backwards and upside-down, and, finally, upside-down. Schillinger goes on to show how in the first eight bars of the original Invention (ex. 2.2) the theme "fall[s] into the triple repetition of an insignificant melodic pattern." This could have been avoided had Bach used Schillinger's "method of geometrical inversion" to "obtain the . . . version of thematic continuity" shown in Example 2.3.

Seven forms of 4 - 19

EXAMPLE 2.4

For the terrestrial musicologist, the repeated juxtaposition of the major scale and the Phrygian mode within the same octave, without modulation or transition of any sort, and the curious emphasis on the subdominant triad (the inversional substitute for the tonic triad—if only we could hear its fifth as a root!) seem more problematical than Bach's "triple repetition of an insignificant melodic pattern."

Martian musicology seems still to be inadequate for the analysis of our music where the works it addresses are more ambiguous and problematic in their relation to the traditional major-minor tonal system. Take, for instance, the beginning of Liszt's *Faust Symphony* (ex. 2.4), which has frequently been cited as an illustration of how a chromatic succession of augmented triads stretches the bounds of traditional tonality. Allen Forte disputes the conventional wisdom of this interpretation because "not one of these analyses incorporates the opening *ab* in violas and cellos, which is marked *ff* and is to be played with downbow."[3] He resolves this discrepancy by interpreting the first four notes as a representation of a special tetrachord—identified as "4-19" in a catalog of pitch-class sets provided by Mr. Forte—and the example as a whole as a series of overlapping inverted and transposed transformations of this tetrachordal collection.

It is precisely the most characteristic features of a language that are

[3]Allen Forte, "Liszt's Experimental Idiom and Music of the Early Twentieth Century," *19th Century Music* X/3 (Spring 1987): 217.

likely to be taken for granted and left unexplained by those who speak it, and thus someone who brings a fresh approach—the Martian musicologist who doesn't know that the *Eroica* is "tonal"—may sometimes alert us to an important detail that has been overlooked precisely because it is so all-pervasive. Forte calls attention to the special emphasis that Liszt gives to the hitherto neglected first note of the *Faust Symphony*, but it is not at all evident that this emphasis implies that Liszt heard it, or expected us to hear it, simply as another component of a tetrachordal cell that includes the following augmented triad and that is supposed to generate what everyone has always taken to be exactly what it seems to be—a chromatic succession of augmented triads. Doesn't it seem more reasonable to suppose that this emphasis has the opposite intention: to set that *ab* apart? This, at any rate, seems to have been its effect, according to Forte himself, on everyone else who has analyzed this passage. The hitherto neglected *ab* is, in fact, as he points out, an especially important note, but what is important and special about it utterly disappears in his analysis. Isn't it better to explain that initial *ab* as initiating a chromatic descent—*ab-g-f#-f-e*—in which the last four notes but not the first are each embellished so that we have a parallel descent of the four augmented triads, and to show how that *ab* imparts priority and a sense of closure to the last of these augmented triads, which encompasses the major third outlined by the descent of·*ab* to *e*? This is how I, at any rate, would reply to Forte's challenge as to the initial *ab*, even if I knew nothing more of the work than the citation given above in Example 2.4. It is enlightening to compare that citation, which is taken from Forte, with the following quotation of the opening bars as given in a standard harmony text (ex. 2.5).[4] This should be enough to make us wonder about the provenance of an analytic method that establishes

[4]Walter Piston, *Harmony*, 5th ed., rev. by Mark DeVoto (New York: W. W. Norton, 1987), p. 439.

EXAMPLE 2.5   Liszt, Faust Symphony

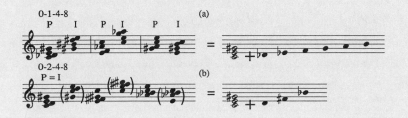

EXAMPLE 2.6

an inclusion relation between the initial *ab* and the *g-b-eb* augmented triad simply because they are contiguous, but not between that *ab* and the *e-g#-c* augmented triad, whose tonal priority in this passage must surely always have been self-evident to less esoteric musicologists.

Forte might object to the a priori tonal connotations of the term "augmented triad" to designate the 0-4-8 trichord, which he identifies by its catalog number, "3-12." But his analysis distorts the general implications of that structure, whatever we may choose to call it, as thoroughly as it distorts the specific contextual implications of the initial *ab*. Because of the self-transposability of the 0-4-8 trichord, it can be a component of one or the other of only two tetrachordal collections (ex. 2.6): the 0-1-4-8 tetrachord deduced by him from the series of "augmented triads"[5] in Example 2.4, or the 0-2-4-8 tetrachord. Forte's analysis of the opening of the *Faust Symphony* is trivial, for the

[5]See n. 16, Chapter I. (I will generally not add quotation marks to terms borrowed from the traditional nomenclature for use in a non-traditional context, but I request the reader to remember that they are implied.)

simple reason that it is equally relevant to *any* progression of an augmented triad to a transposition of itself by *any* interval that contains
an odd number of semitones. Any such juxtaposition of two augmented triads will generate overlapping 0-1-4-8 tetrachords exactly
as Example 2.4 does. Indeed, any note at all that stands next to an
augmented triad of which it is not a component *must* form, with that
triad, one or the other of only two tetrachordal types. The mere determination of whether the resultant tetrachord is Forte Catalog No.
4-19 or Forte Catalog No. 4-24 is not, in itself, an insightful analytical
perception. The value for analysis of what Forte has given us in Example 2.4 is about the same as the value for science of the experiment
conducted by a certain high school sophomore for his general science
class. Asked to establish whether or not it was true that a grasshopper's organ of hearing was located in his legs, he placed the grasshopper on a table, made a loud noise, and the grasshopper jumped;
then he detached the grasshopper's legs, made a loud noise, and the
grasshopper didn't jump.

But this doesn't mean that a composer cannot derive significant
compositional consequences from the precompositional structural relations inherent in tetrachordal collections of which the augmented
triad is a component. It only means that we can never discover these
through Allen Forte's method of analysis, which has no more relevance to music that actually exploits these relations than it has to music that does not, like the opening of the *Faust Symphony*. For an example of the compositional exploitation of the 0-1-4-8 tetrachord I
refer you to Berg's *Wozzeck*. In the *sonata allegro* movement (Act II,
Scene 1) the various harmonic areas are defined and interrelated
through the systematic exploitation of basic cells. The principal one
of these may be defined as an augmented triad plus a conjunct semitone superimposed upon any one of its constituents (ex. 2.7). At the
climax of the development section the principal leitmotiv of the opera

EXAMPLE 2.7

Wir ar – me Leut!

EXAMPLE 2.8

EXAMPLE 2.9

is shown to be a linear statement of this cell and is given at a transposition that retains the content of the augmented triad at its primary referential pitch level in the movement (ex. 2.8).[6]

In the first movement of Schoenberg's Second Quartet, Opus 10, the last work of his tonal period, the figure (ex. 2.9) that Schoenberg's pupil, Erwin Stein, describes in a prefatory note to the score as the "2nd theme" of the "Subsidiary subject" combines, at its first appearance in bar 58, both types of "augmented-triad tetrachords" in its five pitch classes: eb-d-b-g = 0–1–4–8, and eb-f-g-b (or its self-inversional form, g-f-eb-b) = 0–2–4–8. Is it meaningful to call attention to these inclusion relations, or is this another example of Martian musicology? Professor Taruskin supposes that the Martian musicologists "would not know that [the *Eroica*] is 'tonal.' " It might be more relevant to ask

---

[6] George Perle, *The Operas of Alban Berg*. Vol. 1: *Wozzeck* (Berkeley and Los Angeles: University of California Press, 1980), pp. 145–55.

EXAMPLE 2.10 Schoenberg, Op. 10, 2nd mvt.

Copyright 1912 by Universal Edition. Renewed Copyright 1940 by Arnold Schoenberg. Used by permission of Belmont Music Publishers.

what they *would* know. Would they share our perception of octave equivalence? In that case they might also share my perception of the *d* as a "dissonant" element that resolves to the second *eb*. Would they distinguish the *d* in this respect from the *f* of the 0-2-4-8 tetrachord? The harmonic context in which Example 2.9 occurs at its first appearance might offer a clue (ex. 2.10). In the cello part at bars 61–62 we find Schoenberg employing Schillinger's "method of geometrical inversion," but where in its application to the Bach Invention this method drastically distorted the harmonic character of the motive, in this instance it doesn't affect its harmonic character at all. The 0-2-4-8 collection, *eb-f-g-b*, unfolded in the original statement of the motive is reflected in its inversion in a complementary form, *b-a-g-eb*, that is contained in the same five-note segment of a whole-tone scale, *eb-f-g-a-b*. The "dissonant" *d* resolving to the closing *eb* of the prime statement is reflected in the "dissonant" *c* resolving to the closing *b* of the inversion. The missing *c#* of the whole-tone collection is provided in the second bar of Example 2.10, which is limited to another five-note collection of the same scale, *a-b-c#-eb-f*. Since the whole-tone scale is

EXAMPLE 2.11

a symmetrical—i.e., a self-invertible—structure, unlike the F major scale on which the Bach Invention is based, its harmonic sense is not affected by inversion.

In its very next appearance the motive is subjected to the first of a number of small modifications in its original intervallic pattern (ex. 2.11). The fifth note is raised by a half step, and in place of its original descent by a whole step we have a descent by a half step. The change in contour is minimal, but for anyone other than a Martian musicologist that minimal change radically transforms the harmonic character of the motive. The *eb* to *eb* boundary octave that imparted a kind of leading-tone function to the *d* is gone, and where that *d* was originally the only "dissonant" element in what was otherwise a whole-tone structure, this time, thanks to the change of *g* to *ab*, it forms part of another cyclic collection, the diminished-7th chord. If there is again a sense of harmonic closure in the last note of the motive, I would attribute it to the return to that same diminished-7th chord after the passing-note *g* between that last note and the preceding *ab*. If now, in Example 2.12, we restore the transformed motive to its immediate context in the quartet, we find this interpretation confirmed in a third version of the antecedent segment of the motive, assigned to the second violin part. Again, the change in contour is minimal. The first note of the figure is lowered, relative to the others, by a semitone, and this minimal revision entirely converts the figure into a linear statement of the diminished-7th chord. A vertical statement of the same chord occurs on the third beat of bar 62. In bars 63–

EXAMPLE 2.12

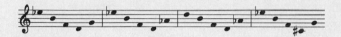

EXAMPLE 2.13

65 we return to the whole-tone collection, linearly represented in the second violin by still another minimal transformation of the antecedent segment. The whole series of transformations is shown in Example 2.13, where all four versions are given in the same register to facilitate comparison. The complete whole-tone collection is finally presented without any simultaneous "dissonant" element (the *d* in bars 63 and 64) in the last four eighth-note values of Example 2.12.

If we have analyzed these first appearances of the "2nd theme" of the "Subsidiary subject" without referring them to the larger context implied in the key signature of F♯ minor we see in the examples, it is because they have a self-contained character within that larger context which not only permits but demands such an analysis. The augmented triad, the whole-tone scale, and the diminished-7th chord are cyclic and symmetrical structures that play an ambiguous and problematical role in late tonal music, and if we are to understand that role we have first of all to recognize them for what they are in and of them-

EXAMPLE 2.14

selves. Only in the closing bars of the movement is the motive shown in Example 2.9 at last subjected to a transformation that unambiguously refers it to the principal tonality (ex. 2.14).

Having nothing to tell us about the meaning of these transformations of the theme, the Martian analyst is content to give us a statistical report:

[Maegaard] counts forty-eight statements of the . . . motive and its variants in the first movement of Schoenberg's Second Quartet. . . . [He] calls this initial form [ex. 2.9] the "Grundgestalt" and translates it into interval-number notation as follows: $-4-6-3+5-2-2$. Each of the twenty-seven variants is similarly notated. Transpositions are not identified and there is not a word about the harmonic implications of the different forms of the motive. . . . The harmonic meaning of [Example 2.14] counts for nothing in the analysis, which tells us only that among the twenty-eight forms the one whose interval-number representation is $-3-6-4+5-2-2$ occurs five times. This kind of motivic analysis is problematical enough in atonal music, where the harmonic context justifies the use of interval numbers rather than qualitative interval names and where the harmonic implications of different transpositions and variants of a given motive are far more ambiguous. Applied to a tonal composition, it takes us into a musical wonderland where we would not distinguish between the following melodies, since in both of them a "Grundgestalt" is transformed into the "same" variant [ex. 2.15].

EXAMPLE 2.15

Even if [Example 2.9] and its variants had been properly described and compared, a table of the number of occurrences of each
would contain no significant information. What generalizations are
we supposed to derive from this data? The relative importance of
the different versions of the motive? Whatever one may mean by
such a question, its answer cannot take a statistical form. Is a single
statement of a motive that effects a striking change of key at a salient moment in the formal design only one quarter as important
as a fourfold repetition of the same motive as an accompaniment
figure? There must be several hundred frequency tables of this sort
among Maegaard's analyses. It is impossible to infer anything from
them, in spite of percentiles calculated to the second decimal place.[7]

Statistical analysis has two practical advantages over pitch-class set
analysis: it is easier to do, and the results can be verified. But as to
what it can tell us about a piece of music, what Professor Taruskin has
had to say on this score about pitch-class set analysis applies equally
to the kind of statistical analysis we have just described. To the argument that Forte's methods are not incompatible with other analytical procedures, Taruskin replies as follows:

Compatibility, not incompatibility, is the issue. For pc set "analysis" is incompatible with nothing, as the fact of its universal poten-

[7]George Perle, review of Jan Maegaard, *Studien zur Entwicklung des Dodekaphonen
Satzes bei Arnold Schönberg* (Copenhagen: Hansen, 1972), in *Musical Quarterly* LXIII/
2 (April 1977): 279f.

tial applicability already testifies. It begins not with observation of musical particulars but with a universe of possibilities. The comparison of any musical entity with such a universe yields an inexhaustible quarry of "true facts" but no criterion of relevance. As long as no such criterion has been established . . . the endless stream of ostensible relations stemming from the pc survey can persuade us for a while that analysis is being accomplished. But in fact it is only a tabulation that can just as well be carried on in the presence of analysis as in its absence (hence the universal "compatibility"). Nor is it really so innocuous as I may be making it seem, since in its anodyne effect (one never comes back from the fishing expedition empty-handed, there is always "something to say," some "finding" to report) it can deflect attention away from the task at hand, which is to formulate analytical methods, not concoct a universal solvent.[8]

We have cited examples of musical analyses which are so irrelevant to our common musical experience as to suggest the possibility that they are the work of extraterrestrial musicologists. I conclude with a converse example—the Martian musicologist revealing the same disconnection from our common musical experience in his novel formulation of concepts that we have always assumed to be universally shared and self-evident.

In his book *The Structure of Atonal Music*, Allen Forte offers a brief description of the beginning of the Second Part of *Le Sacre du printemps*: "The next example of invariants [ex. 2.16] is of interest since it is a very clear illustration of the occurrence of an invariant subset within a small context and since it highlights the essential nature of equivalent sets in a remarkable musical context." The innocent reader who might pause at this point for a glance at the example might very

[8]Taruskin, "Reply to van den Toorn," p. 57.

A : [2, 3, 5, 6, 9, 10]
B : [1, 2, 4, 5, 8, 9]

EXAMPLE 2.16   Stravinsky, *Le Sacre du printemps*

well suppose that the "equivalent sets" to which Forte refers are three instances of the same familiar chord: a sustained D minor triad and, moving in eighth-note motion against this, its chromatic neighbor-note chords, alternate D♯ and C♯ minor triads (or, if we prefer, E♭ and D♭ minor triads—the orchestral score presents both readings simultaneously, the former in the flutes, the latter in the clarinets). But these are not the "equivalent sets" that Forte discerns in this passage. "As is evident in example [2.16], $B = T(A, 11)$. The invariant subset [2, 5, 9] is sustained in dotted half-notes while the remaining elements change. Thus, there is a fluctuation of pitch-class content while interval content remains constant."[9] In other words, what Forte sees as the basis of this excerpt are the two six-note collections that we find when we add together *all* the notes that occur simultaneously: *d e♭ f g♭ a b♭* alternating with the same at the semitone below, *c♯ d e f g♯ a*. And what he supposes to be remarkable about the relation of these two simultaneities is that they share an invariant subset [2, 5, 9], more commonly known as a D minor triad. But Stravinsky doesn't *add* that subset to the residue of each six-note "set." He *subtracts* it, precisely

[9]Allen Forte, *The Structure of Atonal Music* (New Haven: Yale University Press, 1973), p. 35.

by "[sustaining it] in dotted half-notes while the remaining elements change." That this residue is in each instance a transposition of the same subset isn't mentioned by Forte. In fact, the perpetual eighth-note motion persists for twenty-three bars, with one or another transposition—eventually all twelve—of the "subset [2,5,9]" occurring on the eighth-note values. The sustained D minor triad in alternation with an E dominant-7th chord persists through the first fourteen measures of the movement, against this regular eighth-note pattern of exclusively minor triads. Do we really have to look these chords up in Forte's catalog in order to find a name for them? Another theorist assures us that "Allen Forte's perceptive interpretation . . . accounts for an essential quality of this mysteriously pulsating music. The eighth-note chords of the flute and clarinets form alternately, with the sustaining oboes and horns, the six-tone sonorities labeled A and B. The sonorities A and B are both representatives of the same set class (6-Z19) and are thus made up of precisely the same intervals. As Forte points out, 'there is a fluctuation of pitch-class content while interval content remains constant.'"[10] "A fluctuation of pitch-class content while interval content remains constant" is what the rest of us have always known as "a transposition."

This is the sort of analysis that now characterizes much of what passes for contemporary music theory in our colleges and in our professional journals. How are we to account for the general defenselessness of our academic music departments in the face of this invasion by "a troop of Martian musicologists"?

The crucial and monumental development in the art music of our century has been the qualitative change in the foundational premises of our musical language—the change from a highly chromaticized

[10]Christopher Hasty, in a review of Piston (DeVoto), *Harmony*, in *Journal of Music Theory* XXVI/1 (Spring 1982): 164.

tonality whose principal functions and operations are still based on a limited selection, the seven notes of the diatonic scale, from the universal set of twelve pitch classes to a scale that comprehends the total pitch-class content of that universal set. We can point to the moment of that change with some precision. It occurs most obviously in the music of Scriabin and the Vienna circle, Schoenberg, Webern, and Berg, in 1909–1910, and very soon afterwards, though less obviously, in the music of Bartók and Stravinsky. I think it is safe to say that nothing comparable in significance to this transformation in the basic material of the language of music has occurred since the beginnings of polyphony. I would go even further and say that nothing of comparable significance for music has *ever* occurred, because the closing of the circle of fifths gives us a symmetrical collection of all twelve pitch classes that eliminates the special structural function of the perfect fifth itself, which has been the basis of every real musical system that we have hitherto known.

The revolutionary character of this transformation in the tone material disoriented not only the theorists and historians of the new music, but the very composers in whose works this transformation was implemented. His need to establish analogies between the new music and the classical tradition led Schoenberg, for example, to the most startling assertions about his own music in his only extended exposition of twelve-tone composition.[11] An "irregularity" in the order of the notes of the series in Opus 25 is justified by the fact that it occurs in the second movement, when "the set has already become familiar." But similar "irregularities" occur throughout the first movement as

[11]Arnold Schoenberg, "Composition with Twelve Tones," in *Style and Idea: Selected Writings of Arnold Schoenberg*, ed. Leonard Stein (New York: St. Martin's Press, 1975), pp. 214–45, based on a lecture given at Princeton in 1934 which was substantially revised in 1941 and first published in *Style and Idea*, ed. Dika Newlin (New York: Philosophical Library, 1950). My comments on this essay are taken from my review of the 1975 edition in *Musical Quarterly* LXVII/3 (July 1976): 439f.

well. There is not a single twelve-tone piece of Schoenberg's to which the following statements by the composer himself can be shown to have any reasonable application whatever: "One could perhaps tolerate a slight digression [in the order of the notes] in the later part of a work, when the set had already become familiar to the ear. However, one would not thus digress at the beginning of a piece"; and "While a piece usually begins with the basic set itself, the mirror forms and other derivatives, such as the eleven transpositions of all the four basic forms, are applied only later." Where the set is segmented into chords at the beginning of a piece, as it very often is, we can only know the ordering of the chords, not the ordering of the notes within each chord. Thus the three chords which open the Piano Piece, Opus 33a, can represent any one of 13,824 (=4!×4!×4!) different twelve-tone series. And this first set-statement is *immediately* followed by a "mirror" form, which may be interpreted as the retrograde-inversion of any one of these, since it too is partitioned into three four-note chords. The systematic association of the basic set with one of its "mirror" forms, the inversion, begins to appear as early as 1925, and from 1928 to the end of his life almost every composition of Schoenberg's consistently pairs the basic set with a given transposition of the inversion. In fact, the assertion that an inversion would be "applied only later" is explicitly contradicted elsewhere in the article itself.

The inversion of a theme in tonal music is an optional compositional device; the invertibility of a twelve-tone set is a precompositional premise of the system. The former occurs in an a priori harmonic context which establishes the frame of reference; the latter is *itself* the source of foundational pitch relations. The former is never literal, the latter invariably so. As a composer Schoenberg could not and did not equate inversion and the other basic transformation procedures of twelve-tone composition with contrapuntal thematic procedures in tonal music; as a theorist he continually reverts to such an equation, citing Bach, Beethoven, and "the masters of contrapuntal times" as offering antecedents for his own practice. It is not surprising that his critics, those who were hostile as well as those who were friendly, should have argued from the same premises. Thus, for example, we find one of the latter referring to a "pre-harmonic contrapuntal consciousness based on the notion of horizontal, not vertical, polyphony," and suggesting that "the idea of Netherlandish polyphony emerges more and more distinctly as one proceeds into the examination of Webern's compositions."[12] In fact, as Rognoni must surely have known, that "pre-harmonic contrapuntal consciousness," through its rigorous control of intervallic simultaneity, produced the most triadically consonant music we have ever known.

It was Webern who drew the most radical and distinctive inferences from the displacement of the diatonic scale by the universal set of twelve non-functional pitch classes, in "music on the edge of nothingness, music of an unprecedented brevity, stillness, and tension, in which a single note or chord could constitute a 'theme,' in which every trace of padding and doubling and even the very concept of harmonic 'background' or 'accompaniment' had been eliminated. It was even suggested that Webern had invented a new musical entity, the 'pensato,' a note which was to be imagined, not played."[13] In spite of its extreme economy of means, which results in a texture that rarely involves simultaneities of more than two or three notes, Webern's is music of extraordinary density in its structure and interrelations. The brevity of his compositions is therefore not an idiosyncratic charac-

---

[12]Luigi Rognoni, *The Second Vienna School*, trans. Robert W. Mann (London: Calder, 1977), p. 346. See my review in the *Times Literary Supplement*, May 26, 1978.

[13]George Perle, review of Hans Moldenhauer and Rosaleen Moldenhauer, *Anton von Webern: A Chronicle of His Life and Work* (New York: Knopf, 1979), in the *Washington Post*, April 8, 1979.

teristic, but one that is inseparably correlative to every other feature of his compositional language. Yet Webern, himself a conductor, was loath to admit the degree to which his music differed from that of other composers in its relation to the dimension of time and habitually attributed durations to his works that were two or three times longer than what is to be unmistakably inferred from his very explicit and exhaustive metronome markings. Writing to Schoenberg soon after completing the Symphony, Op. 21, he reports that the first movement "lasts almost a quarter of an hour" and the second "about six minutes." If we are to respect his own metronome markings, the first movement cannot last longer than about six minutes and the second movement no longer than about two.[14]

By the time of his Fourth String Quartet, inversional symmetry had become as fundamental a premise of Bartók's harmonic language as it is of the twelve-tone music of Schoenberg, Berg, and Webern. Neither he nor they ever realized that this connection establishes a profound affinity between them in spite of the stylistic features that so obviously distinguish his music from theirs. In an essay published immediately after his completion of the Fourth Quartet, Bartók emphasizes that distinction:

> Our peasant music, naturally, is invariably tonal, if not always in the sense that the inflexible major and minor system is tonal. (An "atonal" folk-music, in my opinion, is unthinkable.) Since we depend upon a tonal basis of this kind in our creative work, it is quite self-evident that our works are quite pronouncedly tonal in type. I must admit, however, that there was a time when I thought I was

[14]The letters to Schoenberg are quoted in Moldenhauer and Moldenhauer, *Anton von Webern*, pp. 325f., who infer, from the discrepancies between Webern's assertions regarding their durations and their actual performance times, that certain works "are played almost twice as fast" as they should be.

EXAMPLE 2.17

EXAMPLE 2.18

approaching a species of twelve-tone music. Yet even in works of that period the absolute tonal foundation is unmistakable.[15]

Nowhere does he recognize the communality of his harmonic language with that of the twelve-tone composers that is implied in their shared premise of the harmonic equivalence of inversionally symmetrical pitch-class relations.

I have shown elsewhere how this communality is explicitly expressed in the way that Berg in *Lulu* and Bartók in the Fourth and Fifth Quartets exploit the same basic cell, a four-note collection comprising two tritones separated by either a perfect fourth, or, equivalently, a minor second (ex. 2.17).[16] This cell is symmetrical, i.e., self-invertible, which is to say that it may be inverted without change of its pitch-class content. In Example 2.18 the twelve-tone scale is laid out as an array of inversionally complementary pitch classes. If we take *bb* and *a* to be inversionally complementary to each other, then

[15]Béla Bartók, "The Folk Songs of Hungary," *Pro Musica* VII (October 1928). Reprinted in Béla Bartók, *Béla Bartók Essays*, ed. Benjamin Suchoff (New York: St. Martin's Press, 1976), pp. 338f.

[16]George Perle, "The First Four Notes of *Lulu*," in Douglas Jarman, ed., *The Berg Companion* (London: Macmillan, 1989).

EXAMPLE 2.19

so are *eb* and *e*. I call such inversionally complementary pairs "P/I dyads."[17] From either of these P/I dyads we can deduce the inversional complement of any other note of the twelve-tone scale. Such an array may be defined by its axis of symmetry, i.e., the points of intersection at which the same P/I dyad is repeated. But another interpretation of this same four-note collection is possible. We can replace either note of each of these P/I dyads by its tritone to form an alternative pair of symmetrically related dyads: *e* and *a*, *eb* and *bb*. In this new interpretation the same four-note cell becomes a member of a second array of P/I dyads, at a minor-3rd transposition of the original array (ex. 2.19). Conversely, either of these arrays may be represented by the minor-3rd transposition of the same cell (ex. 2.20). The structural implications that may be derived from the properties of this basic cell of Berg's *Lulu* and of Bartók's Fourth and Fifth Quartets—properties which it shares only with the other two tetrachords that are divisible into tritones, the French 6th and the diminished-7th chords—are the same for both composers.

Bartók did not choose to discuss his music in analytical terms, but Berg did do so on occasion, and his own version of the derivation of the basic cell of *Lulu* from the basic series of the opera is illustrated in an example he prepared for his "authorized" biographer, Willi

[17]Perle, "Berg's Master Array of the Interval Cycles," *Musical Quarterly* LXIII/1 (January 1977): 6f.

EXAMPLE 2.20

EXAMPLE 2.21

Reich (ex. 2.21).[18] It is, perhaps, not fair to attribute to Berg himself Reich's confused interpretation of the eight-note residue that remains after the "Quartenmotif" is extracted from the basic series. What the example shows is that we can extract from this residue a second statement of the "Quartenmotif" and that this will leave another basic four-note cell, the diminished-7th chord. Together the three beamed tetrachords give us one of the three basic twelve-tone tropes of the opera (ex. 2.22), which is nowhere mentioned in Reich's "analysis." The primary basic cell generates another, more important, twelve-tone trope, which Reich also fails to cite (ex. 2.23). But the primary basic cell is principally employed as an independent motive whose

[18]Willi Reich, *Alban Berg. Mit Bergs eigenen Schriften und Beiträgen von Theodor Wiesengrund Adorno und Ernst Krenek* (Vienna: Herbert Reichner, 1937), Example 52 and p. 113.

EXAMPLE 2.22

EXAMPLE 2.23

EXAMPLE 2.24   Berg, *Lulu*

Act II, Copyright 1964 by Universal Edition A.G., Wien. Revision © Copyright 1985 by Universal Edition A.G., Wien. Act III, Copyright 1977, 1978 by Universal Edition A.G., Wien. All Rights Reserved. Used by permission of European American Music Distributors Corporation, sole U.S. and Canadian agent for Universal Edition A.G., Wien.

signal character throughout the opera, like its large-scale structural implications, also derives from its divisibility into two tritones. However we unfold this motive, it falls into two identical or complementary intervals (ex. 2.24). Precisely the same property accounts for the signal character of the same four-note cell in the Fifth Quartet of Bartók. The failure of Berg's derivation procedure (ex. 2.21) to ac-

count for the frequent employment of the primary basic cell independently of the twelve-tone trope thus derived (ex. 2.22) casts doubt
on the validity of the procedure itself. But there is an even stronger
reason for questioning its validity. We can derive the twelve-tone set
shown in Example 2.22 by applying exactly the same derivation procedure to any one of the 479,001,600 permutations of the twelve-tone
scale. And if Bartók was less misleading than Berg on the subject of
the special structural implications of the basic cell of the Fourth and
Fifth String Quartets, it was only because, so far as we know, he never
said anything at all about it.

There are other composers of the revolutionary generation who
could perhaps have explained their work in more relevant terms but
who chose to remain silent. According to a contemporary of his,
"Scriabin always said that everything in his later compositions was
strictly according to 'law.' He said that he could prove this fact. However, everything seemed to conspire against his giving a demonstration. One day he invited Taneyev and me to his apartment so he could
explain his theories of composition. We arrived and he dilly-dallied
for a long time. Finally, he said he had a headache and would explain
it all another day. That 'another day' never came."[19] Van den Toorn's
exhaustive study has established the pervasive, persistent, and essential role in Stravinsky's oeuvre of systematic interactions between diatonic elements and a symmetrical scale of alternating whole steps and
half steps.[20] In his memoirs Rimski-Korsakov describes his discovery
of what is now known as the "octatonic scale."[21] Yet nowhere in his

---

[19]Faubion Bowers, *The New Scriabin* (New York: St. Martin's Press, 1973), p. 129.
[20]Pieter C. van den Toorn, *The Music of Igor Stravinsky* (New Haven: Yale University Press, 1983).
[21]Nikolai Rimski-Korsakov, *My Musical Life*, trans. Judah A. Joffe (London: Eu-
lenberg Books, 1936), p. 72. The term "octatonic scale" was introduced by Arthur
Berger in "Problems of Pitch Organization in Stravinsky," *Perspectives of New Music*
II/1 (Fall–Winter 1963).

writings or in the six volumes of his "conversations" with Robert Craft does Stravinsky, in spite of numerous generous references to his teacher, ever acknowledge this central feature of his own musical language and his indebtedness to Rimski-Korsakov for it. One can only conclude, with Richard Taruskin, that "Stravinsky always guarded his technical advances and innovations as trade secrets,"[22] and it seems reasonable to suppose that the same attitude also explains Scriabin's refusal to discuss his own, very different, exploitation of the same scale.

If the composers who made the revolution chose not to or were unable to discuss the respects in which their music represented a radical transformation of the tone material, they so much took for granted those respects in which composing, for them, was still what it had always been that it could never have occurred to them to say anything about these self-evident and obvious matters. They would not have understood the advantage of discussing their harmonic language in terms of "simultaneities" rather than "chords," in terms of "pitch classes" rather than "pitches." Their own experience with the meaning of "simultaneity" in tonal music imposed certain responsibilities upon them when they were faced with the problem of "simultaneity" in post-tonal music. They continued to concern themselves with questions of voice-leading, octave displacement, and doubled chord-tones, which meant that they composed with "pitches," or even "notes," rather than "pitch classes." As a tonal composer Scriabin had been in the habit of distinguishing between identical "pitch-class collections" such as dominant-7th chords and German 6th chords, not only in their compositional functions but in their notation as well. Despite the discrepancy between a new musical

[22]Richard Taruskin, "Chronomor to Kashchei: Harmonic Sorcery; or, Stravinsky's 'Angle,'" *Journal of the American Musicological Society* XXXVIII/1 (Spring 1985).

language based on the twelve-tone scale and a traditional notation derived from the seven degrees of the diatonic scale, Scriabin continued to employ consistent and uniform rules of notation, thus providing us with an indispensable key to the analysis of his later works.[23]

The fundamental change in the language of music has given rise to a special terminology. It makes more sense to describe the arrays of P/I dyads illustrated in Examples 2.18 and 2.19 as differing in pitch level by "interval-3" rather than as differing by "a minor third." Schoenberg, as a composer, understood very well that inversional complementation in his twelve-tone music was an operation affecting pitch-class rather than pitch relations. Had he also understood this as a theorist he would, perhaps, have been less likely to draw invalid analogies with thematic operations in earlier music. Nevertheless, discussions of musical entities in terms of their "pitch-class content" tend to eliminate every other question—vertical ordering, spacing, pitch doublings, voice leading, octave displacement. To whatever extent these continue to have meaning in contemporary composition, it is still useful to talk about "notes" rather than "pitch classes."

We have an unprecedented situation today: a "classical" repertory of music by twentieth-century composers—Scriabin, Bartók, the Viennese atonalists, Stravinsky, Varèse—whose generational distance from a composer in, let us say, his thirties or forties today, is comparable to that of Brahms and his contemporaries from Mozart and Beethoven. Yet the "classical" figures of the modernist movement in music, the mainstream composers of the twentieth century, remain, on the eve of the twenty-first, problematical and controversial as to the substance and meaning of the foundational elements of their musical language, as Mozart and Beethoven certainly were not to Brahms and his generation. Forty years ago Roger Sessions described

---

[23]See George Perle, "Scriabin's Self-Analyses," *Music Analysis* III/2 (July 1984).

his own generation as one that was, in comparison to these "mainstream" composers of our century, "not at all in the same sense a revolutionary one. It is rather one in which the materials yielded by the revolution must be assimilated anew and given new shapes; one in which the revolution must be appraised and consolidated, in which its various elements must be regrouped and its problems provided with fresh solutions."[24] This task requires first of all that we recognize the common ground of those who made the revolution, a common ground which they themselves failed to recognize. Without an understanding of their connections with each other we can have no real understanding of their connections with us. Without such connections we are without tradition, and without tradition we are without language. Without language, what are we?

[24]Roger Sessions, *The Musical Experience of Composer, Performer, Listener* (Princeton: Princeton University Press, 1950; reprint ed., New York: Atheneum, 1962), p.113.

LECTURE III "Windows of Order"

I hope I have established the futility of the excursions into musicology, from electronics and mathematics respectively, by the inventor of the "Digionic Synthesizer" and by Joseph Schillinger.[1] I do not propose to expose myself to similar hazards by straying beyond the limits of my own very specialized professional education and experience. These cautionary remarks are offered by way of a preface to my explanation of the title of this lecture.

I was startled to find, in a headline on the science page of the *New York Times* of February 12, 1980, an expression that I had been regularly employing for many years in my lectures on early atonal music: "Order Amid Chaos." There is already something about this in the first edition (1962) of *Serial Composition and Atonality*: "In the perpetually changing tone weft of the 'athematic' style any recognizably consistent feature, regardless of its brevity, becomes a structural element." The reference in this instance was to the third piece of Schoenberg's Opus 11, but it is in connection with the very different, and very thematic, first piece of Opus 11 that I mainly presented this concept of the structural role of "any recognizably consistent feature" in giving some coherence to music whose harmonic character, at the

[1] For an evaluation of Schillinger's competence in mathematics see John Backus,

least, seems chaotic compared to that of the "common practice" that preceded it.

Varieties of programmed chaos have been a regular part of the avant-garde scene for a long time now—chance music, aleatoric music, stochastic music, ambient music, etc.—and are themselves a response to the musical chaos unintentionally achieved, sometimes by the very same composers, by more difficult and time-consuming ratiocinative procedures. In the second scene of Berg's *Lulu*, Alwa unexpectedly appears with important news for his father, editor-in-chief of a newspaper: "A revolution has broken out in Paris!" Dr. Schön, however, is preoccupied at the moment: he is trying to force open the door behind which Lulu's husband has just cut his throat. Alwa continues, "No one at the editor's desk knows what to write," to an ordering of the twelve notes that seems to have no relevance whatever to his characteristic tone row, or to any other of the twelve-tone sets on which the opera is based. A chaotic arrangement of the twelve notes would seem to be an appropriate musical metaphor for the sense of his words, but, with Berg, the more obvious the metaphor the more likely it is that the composer will have hidden a second and even more appropriate metaphor beneath it. The patient and persistent analyst will eventually discover that this seemingly disordered twelve-tone aggregate unfolds Alwa's set in a strictly ordered cyclically permuted inversion and, at the same time, a strictly ordered cyclically permuted transposed retrograde-inversion, a serial procedure which only a twelve-tone composer who does not know what to write could contrive, and one which is altogether uncharacteristic of Berg's twelve-tone language and is particularly inconsistent with the way Alwa's series is employed everywhere else in the work. In fact, a revolution has broken out in music, and the problem of not knowing what to write is still with us. Whether one responds to this problem with chance procedures or with extraordinarily abstract and complicated serial operations will not necessarily make any significant difference. An authority on modern music, writing from a different point of view, has put it this way:

> Aleatory structures can, indeed, be seen as peculiarly appropriate to atonal music in general. The creation of musical works without tonal harmony had been a problem for half a century, ever since the first atonal works of Schoenberg, for with the loss of tonality had come the loss of the means for creating goal-directed forms, these means depending on the tonal phenomena of preparation, modulation and resolution. Schoenberg, Webern, Stockhausen and Boulez had all tried various ways of getting around this problem; aleatory composition now allowed it to be ignored.[2]

Let us return to Opus 11 and consider the first movement in the context of its time, before it had yet occurred to anyone that the threat of harmonic chaos implied in the loss of tonality could be ignored. In my last lecture I showed how an episode from the first movement of Schoenberg's preceding opus, the Second String Quartet, in F♯ minor, stretches the bounds of tonality. Those bounds are nevertheless very clearly established and confirmed. The referential function of the principal key is clearly defined in the opening and closing bars of the movement (ex. 3.1), and there is never any doubt about the role of that key in establishing its structural unity. A single chord-type, the triad, still dominates the harmonic texture, all other simultaneities are dissonant relative to it, and there is, ultimately, no ambiguity about the centricity of the tonic note and the tonic triad. The harmonic language of the first movement of Opus 10 is still the harmonic language of the quartets of Beethoven and Schubert.

Opus 11, No. 1 was completed only seventeen months later, on

[2]Paul Griffiths, *Modern Music: A Concise History from Debussy to Boulez* (New York: Thames and Hudson, 1985), p. 178.

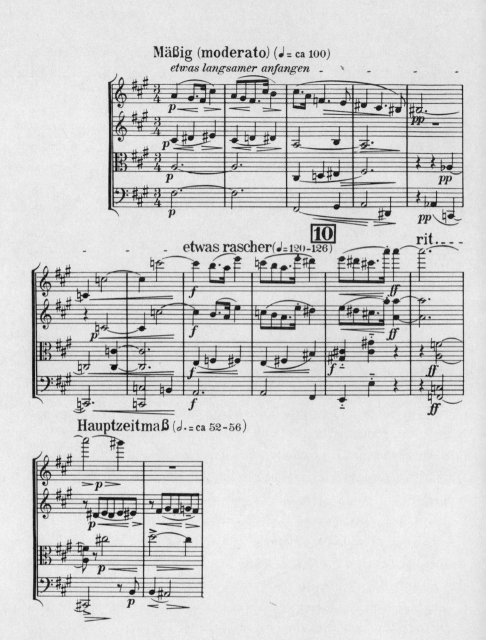

EXAMPLE 3.1(a)   Schoenberg, Op. 10, 2nd mvt.

Copyright 1912 by Universal Edition. Renewed Copyright 1940 by Arnold Schoenberg. Used by permission of Belmont Music Publishers.

EXAMPLE 3.1(b)   Schoenberg, Op. 10, 4th mvt.

February 19, 1909. The basically triadic texture of Example 3.1 has been replaced by unrelievedly and unresolvably dissonant chords; the most characteristic harmonic intervals are the tritone and major seventh, rather than the perfect fifth and major or minor third; and there is no sense of tonic centricity, not even when we arrive at the final chord of the piece (ex. 3.2).

The rhetoric and design of the work are not unfamiliar, however. We immediately recognize bars 9–11 of Example 3.2 as a varied restatement of the first three bars. Rhythmically the two phrases are identical. In both a melodic pattern assigned to the uppermost voice is accompanied by two three-note chords occurring at the same attack points in their respective phrases. The melodic contour in the first statement of the theme, so far as direction is concerned, is repeated in its second statement, except for the change of direction to the closing note of the phrase in the second statement. The intervals that span adjacent notes of the melody are, however (except at the close) increasingly expanded in the second statement, and the interval content of the accompanying chords is drastically revised. We can recognize all these similarities and differences intuitively even upon a first hearing, but we can also recognize something more, something that es-

EXAMPLE 3.2(a)   Schoenberg, Op. 11, No. 1

Copyright 1910 by Universal Edition. Renewed Copyright 1938 by Arnold Schoenberg. Used by permission of Belmont Music Publishers.

tablishes a more momentous connection with earlier music than the affinities in rhetoric and design.

A manual on twelve-tone composition finds an analogy between melody and the twelve-tone row, in that melodies, too, "will constitute ordered successions of tones."[3] But insofar as pitch is concerned, it is only in its contour that the melody in bars 9–11 is similar to the melody in the first three bars. The extent of their dissimilarity

[3]Charles Wuorinen, *Simple Composition* (New York: Schirmer Books, 1979), pp. 22f.

EXAMPLE 3.2(b)

EXAMPLE 3.3

as "ordered successions of tones" is demonstrated in Example 3.3. No transposition of the one will duplicate more than two order positions of the other. It is also contour rather than pitch or interval order that defines the two figures in Example 2.15a as variants of the same motive, since they, too, are dissimilar as "ordered successions of tones," and it is contour rather than pitch or interval order that determines similarity in general between pitch successions in tonal music.

The Martian musicologist is not concerned with whatever it was that motivated Bach to vary these two statements of the same motive, but if the theme of his fugue commences as shown in Example 2.15a rather than as shown in Example 2.15b, there is a reason. Change always takes place against a background structure in tonal music, and that background structure constrains and directs the composer's treatment of motives. Having chosen to unfold the first statement of his motive within the bounds of the fifth and first degrees of the G minor scale, he complements that statement with a variant that will fit into the smaller compass between the octave and the fifth degree.

But Schoenberg's composition is based on a symmetrical twelve-tone scale which presents no such constraints. What motivated Schoenberg to vary his theme in the way that he does? Is there a background structure to explain the change in bars 9–11? I think our ears will tell us that there is, even on a first hearing. One immediately recognizes that the last note in bar 10 is "dissonant" in the sense that it is foreign to the collection of notes that precede it in the same phrase. It is impossible to make similar judgments in the first, expository statement, of this principal subject of the movement. It turns out that the variant form in bars 9–11 can be partitioned into segments of the two whole-tone partitions of the twelve-tone scale, which we can call, in terms of their pitch-class numbers with *c* represented as 0, the

EXAMPLE 3.4

even and odd collections, and which we can represent by the symbols $C2_0$ and $C2_1$:[4]

6208	99	(10)
8	5	
4	11	
6	7	

Perhaps one might even hear the closing *bb*, pitch-class 10, as a resolution of the "dissonant" *a*, pitch-class 9, to the missing component of the even whole-tone collection.[5]

Once we discover this explanation for the special harmonic character of bars 9–11 we will eventually see that the first three bars already imply such a partitioning. Not only do these show very much of a preponderance of one of the two whole-tone collections over the other, but the components of the preponderant collection are temporally and spatially clumped together (ex. 3.4). In this clump of pitches we already have a "window of order"—an expression I have borrowed from the recent book *Chaos*, by James Gleick[6]—a "window

[4]See n. 16, Chapter I.

[5]If the *bb* is supposed to supply the missing component of $C2_0$, what about the two missing components, *eb* and *c#*, of $C2_1$? It is at least worth noting that these pitches mark the registral boundaries of the first figure in the following bar (ex. 3.8).

[6]James Gleick, *Chaos* (New York: Viking, 1987), p. 74.

EXAMPLE 3.5   Mahler, Symphony No. 9, 2nd mvt.

EXAMPLE 3.6

of order" which is opened only when we come to the variant version of the principal subject in bars 9–11.

If the whole-tone collection can open a "window of order" in the context of an atonal composition, it can also open a "window of disorder" in the context of the major/minor system. In the first movement of Mahler's *Das Lied von der Erde* the singer's toast to his drinking companions and host is interrupted by the image of an ape howling in a moonlit graveyard, and the return to the home key as they raise their golden cups to drink is interrupted by the crashing descent of a whole-tone scale. A similarly disruptive role is given to the whole-tone scale in the second movement of the same composer's Ninth Symphony. A series of I–V₇ chords successively transposed through the octave by descending major thirds incidentally unfolds a whole-tone scale in its uppermost line (ex. 3.5). The same passage returns four bars later with this whole-tone scale transposed to the whole step above (ex. 3.6). A whole-tone scale transposed by a whole step or any other even interval number is still the same whole-tone scale, but how are we now to define the chords that make up this progression?

In my first lecture I referred to the special role of the augmented triad in Schoenberg's Opus 11, No. 1. The augmented triad is the characteristic triadic structure of the whole-tone scale, just as the major and minor triads are the characteristic triadic structures of the seven-note diatonic scale.[7] In retrospect we discovered, in the first statement of the principal subject, a "window of order" (ex. 3.4) to the whole-tone partitioning that emerges as a background structure in its variant version at bars 9–11. The latter will, in turn, retrospectively disclose the presence of a second "window of order," the augmented triad (ex. 3.7). That same augmented triad, $C4_0$, is embedded in the following bar (ex. 3.8), in an arpeggio figure that is one of the principal thematic components of the piece. The significance of this invariant relation emerges only gradually. The bracketed segment of Example 3.8, which we will call Subject C, is one of the three principal thematic ideas in the piece. The others, respectively Subjects A and B, are the melody in the first three bars (ex. 3.2a) and the five-

---

[7]I continue to feel uncomfortable about using a term which implies a derivation from the major/minor system, but I prefer this to the imposition of a new terminology on the reader, and especially on the more informed reader to whom "augmented triad" suggests a certain sonorous quality which "C4," though it refers to the same collection, is less likely to evoke. Nevertheless, when I wish to identify the specific rather than the relative pitch-class content of a collection, I will employ the symbols that I have devised for this purpose. Thus, $C4_0$ (equivalent to $C4_4$ and $C4_8$) is the specific "augmented triad" that contains c; $C4_1$ (equivalent to $C4_5$ and $C4_9$), the specific "augmented triad" that contains $c\#$ or db; etc. My analogy between "the augmented triad [as] the characteristic triadic structure of the whole-tone scale" and "the major and minor triads [as] the characteristic triadic structures of the seven-note diatonic scale" should not be taken too literally. The augmented triad, or C4, is a cyclic and symmetrical structure which may be derived by partitioning another such structure, the whole-tone scale, or C2; and the latter, in turn, may be derived by partitioning still another such structure, the semitonal scale, or C1.

EXAMPLE 3.7   Schoenberg, Op. 11, No. 1

Copyright 1910 by Universal Edition. Renewed Copyright 1938 by Arnold Schoenberg. Used by permission of Belmont Music Publishers.

EXAMPLE 3.8

note figure that follows in the left-hand part. Subject C, unlike Subject A or the motive from Bach in Example 2.15a, retains its identity through its relative pitch-class content (or interval structure)[8] rather than through its contour. That content, therefore, is modified only through reordering (ex. 3.9). In this respect it represents a significantly new concept, a first step in the direction of what was to become

[8]Two pitch-class collections have the same "relative pitch-class content" or "interval structure" if either may be transposed or contrapuntally inverted into the other. It is self-evident that two collections that are transpositionally or inversionally equivalent will have the same interval-class content, i.e., the number of instances of each interval class in the one collection will be the same as the number of instances of each interval class in the other. There are, however, certain collections that have, in this sense, the "same" interval-class content (or "interval vectors," in Forte's terminology) but which are nevertheless *not* transpositionally or inversionally equivalent: for example, the four-note collections *a#-b-d-e* and *c-c#-d#-g*, each of which contains a

EXAMPLE 3.9

the twelve-tone set. Subject C is a six-note pitch-class set. (I would not want you to suppose that my rejection of Allen Forte's theory of pitch-class sets implies a rejection of the notion that there can be such a thing as a pitch-class set. It is only when one defines *everything* in terms of pitch-class sets that the concept becomes meaningless.)

If the transformations we see in Example 3.9 at the first and third statements of Subject C can be said to take place in relation to a background structure at all, that background structure is the interval-1 cycle, the symmetrical twelve-tone scale, which presents no such

single instance of each of the six interval classes. Forte assumes that such a relation establishes a compositionally significant criterion of equivalence between two pitch-class collections, even though their respective interval structures are not the same. For example, in one instance we find intervals 1 and 2 derived from four pitch classes (*a#-b/d-e*) and in the other instance from three (*c-c#/c#-d#*). That certain pitch-class collections share the same "interval vector" even though they are neither transpositionally nor inversionally equivalent was first pointed out by Howard Hanson in *Harmonic Materials of Modern Music* (New York: Appleton-Century-Crofts, 1960), p. 22, and by David Lewin in "Re: The Intervallic Content of a Collection of Notes," *Journal of Music Theory* 4:1 (1960). For a general criticism of Forte's concepts of pitch-class set equivalence see Perle, "Pitch-Class Set Analysis: An Evaluation," *Journal of Musicology* 8:2 (1990).

constraints as those that effect motivic variation in tonal music, no basis for such changes in the relative pitch-class content of Subject C as would have been normal and necessary in a diatonic tonal composition. The pitch-class set is one of the consequences of the disappearance of those constraints.

Through its symmetrical partitionings, however, the twelve-tone scale can still provide a basis for change. We have seen that the two whole-tone scales provided a background structure for the transformation of the first statement of Subject A, bars 1–3, into its second statement, bars 9–11. Since Subject C is defined by its relative pitch-class content and not by its contour, it cannot be changed in this way. That content can be transposed, however, and through its symmetrical partitioning into augmented triads the twelve-tone scale provides a basis for Schoenberg's choice of transpositional levels.

Between the two statements of Subject A in bars 1–11 (ex. 3.2a) there is a recurrent five-note figure in the left hand (Subject B) which subsequently also establishes significant associations through the augmented triad. Example 3.10 shows how C_{4_3}, the augmented triad on E♭, is highlighted in a transposed and permuted statement of this figure. In bar 25 of Example 3.10 the same augmented triad initiates a second variant of the first subject. Example 3.11 shows its derivation from the melodic component of the first three bars. In the light of the growing significance of C_{4_3} in bars 22–27 (ex. 3.10), we can see how this same invariant structure determines the new transpositional level of Subject C in bar 28 (ex. 3.9).

In the close of the development section and the transition to the recapitulation (ex. 3.12) we see how the augmented triad determines the overall tonal structure of the movement. Subject C returns in its original arpeggiated form, but at a pitch level that transposes its component augmented triad to C_{4_2} (*f♯-b♭-d*). It is immediately repeated at a major-3rd transposition, which retains the content but permutes

EXAMPLE 3.10

EXAMPLE 3.11

the order of the augmented triad (*a♯-d-f♯*). This is followed by a return of Subject B, restored to its original pitch level—its home key, so to speak—which gives us a third statement of the same augmented triad in the remaining (though interrupted) permutation (*d-f♯-a♯*). And to-gether with this there is a final statement of the melodic component of the first subject, extended to embrace that climactic presentation of all four augmented triads which has been the subject of my special attention and of Professor Cone's as well, and which I discussed in Lecture 1. In the last bar of Example 3.12 we return to $C4_2$, the pitch level at which the augmented triad performs such a strategically im-

EXAMPLE 3.12

EXAMPLE 3.13

portant role in ushering in the closing bars of the movement.[9] So much for "the loss of the means for creating goal-directed forms" and the "various ways of getting around this problem"!

In my first lecture I analyzed the first ten bars of Varèse's *Density 21.5* as unfolding another symmetrical partitioning of the twelve-tone scale, the diminished-7th chord (ex. 3.13). Within these ten bars the octave, *c#-db*, is symmetrically divided by the tritone, and in turn each tritone division, *c#-g* and *g-db*, is itself symmetrically divided by the minor third. This second division gives us another tritone, *e-bb*,

[9]For a discussion of other structural elements in Opus 11, No. 1, see Perle, *Serial Composition and Atonality.*

which must be understood as hierarchically subordinate to the first. The *e* is functionally a passing note between *c♯* and *g*, the *b♭* a passing note between *g* and *d♭*, and while we can see *g* of the first tritone as analogously partitioning *e-b♭*, we do not find *c♯* as a passing note between *a♯* and *e*, or *d♭* as a passing note between *b♭* and *f♭*, since neither *b♭* nor *e* achieves its octave. The notes of this second tritone, *e-b♭*, do not progress beyond their passing-note functions in the first ten bars. My reason for stressing this hierarchical distinction between $C6_1$ and $C6_4$ is that there is a constant shifting of such distinctions, a constant reinterpretation of structural notes as passing notes and vice versa, and it is through this ambiguity, this perpetual change of function, that the composition unfolds. This is what the composition is *about*.

A parenthesis is in order here, on the subject of ambiguity in music, or even in the arts in general. In my earlier discussion of this work I offered, as an alternative to Varèse's own version of bars 8–10, a new interpretation (ex. 1.4) in which the original pitches and rhythm were retained but their presentation altered through the deletion of a *Luftpause*, the substitution of a *crescendo* through all three bars in place of the abrupt dynamic changes in the original, and a revision in modes of attack and articulation implied in my new slurring of the passage. Apart from the fact that it contradicts the composer's intentions, there is nothing inherently wrong in my reconception of how this passage is to be performed. What I have proposed is entirely consistent with what the pitch relations imply: the completion of a cyclic partition of the octave and the consequent move to a new note (*d*) outside that partition. Professor Cone found a discrepancy between the *crescendo* that Schoenberg calls for near the conclusion of Opus 11, No. 1 (ex. 1.2) and the weakening of harmonic tension that results from the reading of a problematical note as *c♯* rather than *b♯*. There is no such discrepancy here. On the contrary, any musically literate person confronted with the notes and rhythms alone and told that dynamics and phrase marks were to be added would very likely find my solution an entirely reasonable one. And that is exactly what is wrong with it! Varèse experiences his discovery of these notes and rhythms "as a child does"—as Sir Peter Medawar puts it in his description of the role of observation in scientific discovery—"without prejudices and preconceptions." I have substituted an adult view of the musical events and eliminated the note of unanticipated triumph upon the attainment of the octave, the sense of frustration and suspense upon the sudden realization of the crisis of continuity that is a consequence of this, the excitement of resolving this crisis in a wilful breakthrough into something new.

Ambiguity is what keeps a work of art alive; it is what gives the listener to a piece of music, the reader of a novel, the viewer of a painting, something to do and makes him a participant in the creation of the work as he hears it, reads it, or looks at it. For Tovey, the second theme of the slow movement of the Fifth Symphony "pauses on a wistful note"; for me it pauses on a questioning one; to neither of us will it sound wistful or questioning in exactly the same way the next time we hear it, for this depends on how we have heard and responded to everything that preceded it, and this can never be exactly the same. In a less great work, what seems ambiguous at first seems less so as we grow increasingly familiar with it. With a work that will last, the ambiguity remains, for it is inherent in the structural relations of the work; it simultaneously confirms and questions the foundational premises of the work. The opening of the *Tristan* Prelude doesn't lose its interest for us after a first hearing, even though we already know that the dominant-7th chord in the third bar is not followed by an A minor triad. Of course, to a less experienced listener a work may be more accessible without the ambiguity than with it, and he may be content to hear it in his own way until that happy moment when he discovers the difference between what the composer had put into it

EXAMPLE 3.14

and what he has gotten out of it. The elderly proprietor of a hardware store I used to patronize was something of a music lover, and occasionally I would hear him humming a tune at his work (ex. 3.14). I once attempted to teach him the original version of this melody, but to no avail. He could only do it his way. We might look with kindly tolerance at this man's mistake, but what about the early conductor of *The Marriage of Figaro* who is supposed to have "corrected" the ambiguity in the first phrase of the overture by repeating the opening bar?

If the sort of ambiguity we speak of is inherent in the structural relations of the work, the listener must be able to recognize the normative implications of those relations. We must assume that the language itself is not so ambiguous to him, as he listens to the Prelude from *Tristan*, that he is altogether insensitive to the harmonic tendencies of the dominant-7th chord. I referred earlier, in connection with Schoenberg's Opus 11, to "the threat of harmonic chaos implied in the loss of tonality," but I have also referred to "the common ground of those who made the revolution" in music. The cyclic partitioning of the semitonal scale—the interval-1 cycle—into interval-2 and interval-4 cycles in Opus 11 and into interval-3 cycles in *Density 21.5* is part of that common ground. In my last lecture I mentioned "the communality of [Bartók's] harmonic language with that of the twelve-tone composers that is implied in their shared premise of the harmonic equivalence of inversionally symmetrical pitch-class relations." It may be "all up," as Leverkühn's Devil puts it, "with the

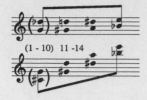

EXAMPLE 3.15

once bindingly valid conventions, which guaranteed the freedom of play," but the common ground of Schoenberg and Varèse, the communality of Bartók and the twelve-tone composers, have their own normative implications, and these can restore "the freedom of play." To the extent that we can define an unambiguous background structure, foreground ambiguity becomes possible.

In bar 11 of *Density 21.5* Varèse breaks out of the closed system of the first ten bars—the diminished-7th chord on *c♯*. The background structure of bars 11–14 is outlined in Example 3.15. Since the tritone repeats itself at the tritone transposition we can read that background structure as a progression through either a series of minor seconds (interval-1) or a series of perfect fifths (interval-1 + interval-6 = interval-7). (As we saw in Example 3.13, however, the tritone partitioned by the minor third and *its* tritone transposition are *not* the same, for they do not encompass the same segment of the interval-3 cycle, and the distinction is a consequential one in *Density 21.5*.) The *d* in bar 11, like the *a* in bar 10 of Opus 11, No. 1, steps into a new harmonic area. The composer reasserts the primacy of the tritone by moving directly to *g♯* but then, carried away by the momentum of this first progression from *c♯-g* to *d-g♯*, he doesn't stop to develop and unfold this second tritone and its octave boundary, as he had taken ten bars to do with the first, but gives us the new *g♯-g♯* octave at once and moves on immediately by another shift of a semitone to a third tritone, *d#-a, both* notes of which are immediately doubled at the octave, and then by still another such shift to a fourth tritone, *bb-e.*

Why does the composer pause upon his arrival at this fourth tritone? Because in all the excitement he suddenly finds himself right back where he had started, in the closed system of the diminished-7th chord C_{3_1}. But there is an important difference. In the context of the unfolding of this harmonic area in bars 1–10, as Example 3.13 demonstrates and as I explained before my digression on the subject of ambiguity, the tritone that brings us back to the "home key" in bar 13 is originally hierarchically inferior to the other tritone of that diminished-7th chord. The *e* emerges merely as a pivot between *c#* and *g,* the *bb* as a pivot between *g* and *db,* and neither component of the *e-bb* tritone attains the octave. But the momentum of the breakthrough in bar 11 carries us back to that hierarchically inferior tritone and lifts it far above everything we've had so far, into an entirely new register, with the interval inverted so that the hierarchically inferior *e* in Example 3.15 bypasses the octave transfer and returns instead at the double octave. This registral superiority is given added emphasis by its temporal prominence at the conclusion of the phrase and by the pause, the longest so far, which marks that conclusion.

But as a consequence of all this the relation between the two tritones of C_{3_1} becomes not less but more ambiguous. Shall we partition the newly exalted *bb-e* tritone with a passing *c#,* just as we had partitioned the original *c#-g* tritone with a passing *e*? Or is the *bb-e* tritone still in its dependent relation? Shall we reinstate the original diminished-7th chord without making any hierarchical distinction this time between the two tritones? The composer decides to leave the tritone gap unfilled for the time being, just as he had left unfilled the two tritones through which he passed on the way to it. The next phrase, bars 15–17, quietly commences with *e* at its bypassed octave position and hovers between its lower and upper semitonal neigh-

EXAMPLE 3.16

EXAMPLE 3.17

bors, but then *f* is replaced by *e♯* and we continue through *f♯* to an octave-displaced *g* in the same register to which we had been brought at the conclusion of the preceding phrase, with that octave displacement compensated for by an octave displacement in the opposite direction for the two chromatic passing notes, *e♯* and *f♯*, that fill in the minor third between the first and last notes of the new phrase. We are left with a piece of unfinished business, a "missing" *c♯*, in the new register attained in bars 13–14 and 17 (ex. 3.16).

In bars 1–5 the tritone is partitioned through the pivotal motion in both directions of its central element, and the ascent from *e* to *g* in bars 14–17 suggests a corresponding descent from *e* to *c♯*. We find this parallelism in the six bars that follow (18–23),[10] but the pivotal motion, unfolding through two registers (ex. 3.17), is from a new note,

[10]The natural sign above the fourth note in bar 23 is my addition. Marc Wilkinson reads this as *b♮* in "An Introduction to the Music of Edgard Varèse," *The Score and I. M. A. Magazine* 19 (1957): 17, as does Harvey Sollberger in his recording of the piece. I think it very likely that this is the correct reading. There is, regardless of whether we read the fourth note as *b♯* or *b♮*, a notational ambiguity here in relation to Varèse's generous use of cautionary accidentals throughout the piece. Compare, for instance, the superfluous sharp inserted before the grace note in bar 30.

EXAMPLE 3.18

b, through which we recover one of the passing tritones, *g#-d*, of bars 11–14 (ex. 3.15).

The work falls into two parts of approximately equal length. The closing section of Part One (bars 24–28) commences with the *e-c#* that we had looked for to balance the *e-g* of bars 13–17, but in a surprising guise and restored to its original register. Though Part One is thus bounded by the principal diminished-7th chord, $C3_1$, it concludes on a question mark. The octave-displaced *d* of bar 21 is restored to its proper place in bars 25–26 and is repeated in the lower octave in bar 27, and partitioning this span is its tritone divider, *g#*. We are left with a new piece of unfinished business, in the failure of the *b* that had been introduced in bars 18–23 as the pivot note between *g#* and *d* to call forth its own tritone associate, *f*—"unfinished business," that is, if we assume that the *g#-b-d* collection represents an incomplete diminished-7th chord, that the work is based on structural relations derived from the interval-3 cycle, and that this implies a tendency for each partition of the cycle to be completely represented. The first half of the piece suggests these hypotheses, and the second half, it seems to me, confirms them.

The only note we have not accounted for in this closing segment of Part One is the last, *eb*, a component of the remaining diminished-7th chord, $C3_0$, a large-scale statement of which, in a series of major sixths rather than minor thirds (ex. 3.18), unfolds through bar 40 of Part Two. A stubbornly intrusive *b* at the climax of this passage (bars

EXAMPLE 3.19   Varèse, *Density 21.5*

© *Copyright 1946 by G. Ricordi & C. SpA, Milano; Copyright Renewed. Reprinted by permission of Hendon Music, Inc., a Boosey & Hawkes Company, Sole Agent. Reprinted by permission*

32–36) finds an affiliate, *d*, only ten bars later (bars 46–50), and the latter brings in its tritone partner, *ab*, but the remaining component of $C3_2$, *f*, is still "missing." With the threefold statement of *c-f#* in the two following bars, the only tritone that has not yet been explicitly stated somewhere in the piece is *b-f*.

The closing section commences on the second beat of bar 53 through the first three beats of bar 56 with a return to the principal diminished-7th chord, $C3_1$, restored to its original register in what is hardly more than a linear reduction of bars 1–7.[11] But if the basic structure—the interval-3 cycle—and the principal "tonality"—the specific partition of that cycle, which may itself be partitioned into two specific interval-6 cycles, *c#-g* and *e-bb*—are so unequivocally confirmed here, it is only to emphasize all the more strongly a reinterpretation of the nucleus of that basic structure, the tritone, a reinterpretation which, commencing with the *c♮* in bar 56, transforms the basic structure itself (ex. 3.19). Where the *bb* in bars 8–9 moved through a passing-note *c* to achieve closure of the $C3_1$ cycle in the octave *c#-db*, in bar 56 the same note moves through a *c* which has been

[11]One note in this passage—the passing note, *a*, in bars 55f.—is registrally displaced and thus acquires a second function, as the symmetrical divider of the *f#-c* tritone in the same register in bars 51f.

displaced to the lower octave (the lowest note in the compass of the instrument, sounded here for the first time) and thence—reiterating on the way the tritone associate e of the $b\flat$—to the d at the major third above. From the second beat of bar 56 through the end of the piece, not only do we find no linear representation of the minor third, the cyclic interval that to this moment has been the structural foundation of the entire work as a pivotal element that either partitions or generates the tritone; the minor third is not even a component of the collective interval content through the second note of bar 59, nor of the collective interval content of the remaining four notes, for in both instances that collective interval content excludes not only the minor third but every other interval that spans an odd number of semitones. Where in Opus 11, No. 1 we recognized a background structure for the first time at bars 9–11, thanks to the partitioning of the pitches into self-contained segments of the two whole-tone scales, here, thanks to this same partitioning, we recognize a *new* background structure. In the former we found "order amid chaos"; here one kind of order replaces another kind.[12] The tritone e-$b\flat$ is now associated with its companion tritones, d-$(g\sharp)$ and c-$f\sharp$, in the whole-tone collection, rather than with its companion $c\sharp$-g of the C3 cycle. There is only one odd melodic interval in Example 3.19, the $f\sharp$-$c\sharp$ which transfers us from $C2_0$ to $C2_1$. And here, in the last two notes of *Density 21.5*, we at last find b paired with its tritone associate. But this last remaining tritone has finally been achieved only as a consequence of

[12]Although both pieces are based on the same ordering principle—the symmetrical partitioning of the twelve-tone scale—they unfold this principle in very different ways and in very different compositional contexts. The Schoenberg piece is, so to speak, much more "chaotic" than the Varèse. It is much more dependent on "thematic associations uniquely characteristic of the given work" (George Perle, *Twelve-Tone Tonality* [Berkeley and Los Angeles: University of California Press, 1977], p. 166). Cf. n. 9, above. The thematic component of *Density 21.5* and its structural role are discussed in the following chapter.

EXAMPLE 3.20

EXAMPLE 3.21

an entirely new harmonic direction that the work takes in its closing bars.

The music of the "common practice" offers many exemplars of such altogether unexpected digressions just as a work is drawing to its close, followed by a return, for the final cadence, to a consequently more emphatic confirmation of the structural relations implied in the body of the work. We can again turn to the slow movement of Beethoven's Fifth Symphony for an analogy with *Density 21.5*. The "echoing afterthoughts" of the end of the first theme draw to a close, after each regular statement of that theme, with the phrase indicated in Example 3.20. In the coda, however, there is a special pathos in the expansion of this phrase at its final leave-taking (ex. 3.21).

Bach provides another striking example at the conclusion of the slow movement of the Brandenburg Concerto No. 2, in the diminished-7th chord progression that interrupts the final cadence (ex. 3.22).

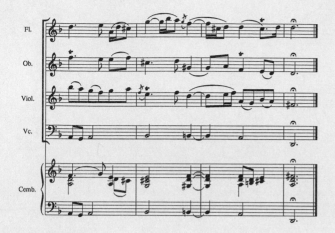

EXAMPLE 3.22

Density 21.5 opened a window for me on a movement of *Le Sacre du printemps* that had frustrated my efforts at analytical understanding for a long time. For a number of years, pending the acquisition of sufficient seniority within the American university system or sufficient prestige in my own specialties outside it to be excused from such basic assignments, a good part of my academic activity was taken up with the teaching of elementary courses in music appreciation. It was, in fact, a rather valuable experience and I gained many insights of which I would otherwise have been deprived. One of the pieces that I invariably included in my repertory was the Introduction to Part One of *Le Sacre*. At some point in my repeated hearings of this music I began to appreciate a detail I had previously overlooked. The A minor melody in the bassoon with which the movement commences (bars 1–3) is heard a second time in a slightly truncated version in bars 7–9 and then, reduced to its head-motive, in bar 13, after which we hear nothing more of this tune until its return at the end of the movement fifty-three bars later. In this last statement, however, it is trans-

EXAMPLE 3.23

posed down by a semitone, unfolding the stepwise descent c♭-b♭-a♭ instead of c-b-a.

Were we to encounter a change in the transpositional level of such a salient theme in the music of Bach, or Beethoven, or Schubert, or Chopin, we would know that the change had certain structural implications and we would try to understand how it was achieved. Why should we assume a more cavalier attitude on Stravinsky's part toward such compositional questions? Surely this transposition must have some structural meaning for the fifty-two intervening bars. What that meaning was continued to puzzle me until I identified the principal subject of those fifty-two bars (ex. 1.13) and realized that, like the first five bars of *Density 21.5*, it partitioned the interval of a tritone into two minor thirds and differentiated these by twice filling in the span of the upper third—first chromatically and then with a single passing note—and leaving the lower third open (ex. 3.23).

Varèse continues into the C3 cycle and thus acquires a second tritone, *e-b♭*, by appending (bars 6–7) an ascending minor third to the higher note of the original tritone. Stravinsky's partitioned tritone is itself the continuation of a C3 cycle, which commences with the bassoon solo's *c-a* head-motive that prefixes the principal subject (ex. 3.24) and then is heard no more until the conclusion of the *più mosso* main body of the Introduction. The two diminished-7th chords are thus unfolded in strikingly different ways, since in the Stravinsky ver-

EXAMPLE 3.24 Stravinsky, *Le Sacre du printemps*

sion the otherwise atonal C3 cycle is initiated by a minor third that is plainly diatonic and tonal, whereas in the Varèse each of the cyclic intervals is consistently and equivalently atonal. This intersecting of inherently non-symmetrical diatonic elements with inherently non-diatonic symmetrical elements seems to me the defining principle of the musical language of *Le Sacre* and the source of the unparalleled tension and conflicted energy of the work.

The transpositional levels assigned to the subject in the course of the movement indicate that the structural plan of the Introduction to Part One of *Le Sacre*, like that of *Density 21.5*, implies the complete representation of each partition of the C3 interval cycle. The first statement of the subject in the bassoon at the beginning of the *più mosso* completes a statement of the $C3_0$ partition (ex. 3.24). The subsequent appearances of the subject are shown in Example 3.25. The $C3_1$ partition commences at No. 4 in the clarinet in D and is completed at No. 8 in the same instrument. Between these two statements of the subject the clarinet in D presents one of the interval-3 components (*e#-d*) of the remaining partition, $C3_2$, in a truncated statement (No. 7) of the subject. At No. 10 the latter is resumed in the clarinet in A, completed by the descent of *d* to *b*, and elaborated through the climactic closing bars of the *più mosso*. With the return to Tempo I at No. 12, $C3_2$ has still been only partially represented, in the partitioned tritone *e#-d-b*. The opening bassoon solo returns, *come*

EXAMPLE 3.25

sopra but at the semitone below, to complete $C3_2$ with the tonal descent from *cb* through *bb* to *ab*.

All this occurs in an immeasurably more complex context in the Stravinsky work, of course. The diatonicism of *Le Sacre du printemps* should not be understood in the restrictive sense of the major/minor system, but in terms of something more basic. Like the symmetrical partitionings of the twelve-tone scale in *Le Sacre*, its diatonicism

> may also be explained in terms of interval cycles—more simply and coherently, in fact, than in terms of the traditional modes and scales. With the single exception of interval[-class] 5, every interval[-class] from 1 through 6 will partition the space of an octave into equal segments. A seven-note segment of the interval-5 cycle, telescoped into the compass of an octave, divides the octave into unequal intervals—"whole-steps" and "half-steps."[13]

[13]Perle, "Berg's Master Array of the Interval Cycles," p. 10.

EXAMPLE 3.26

This interpretation of diatonic collections in *Le Sacre* as telescoped segments of the cycle of fifths is supported by the presence of collections derived from such segments of less and more than seven degrees of the cycle. The five bars that immediately precede the final entry of the principal subject at No. 10 are exclusively based on a four-note segment and, overlapping this, a gapped seven-note segment of the cycle of fifths (ex. 3.26):

e♭ b♭ f c | c g d a e (b) f♯

The entry of the oboe with the *e♭-c* segment of the cycle of fifths is accompanied, after two and three bars, by entries of the clarinet in D, clarinet in B♭, and flute, unfolding various permutations of the same segment and carrying it into the higher octave. The scale figure (ex. 3.27) that ushers in the final statement of the principal subject at No. 10 (ex. 3.25) is restricted to the combined pitch-class content of the overlapping cyclic segments.[14] And with that final statement of the subject we at last arrive at the postponed closing note, *b*, of $C3_2$—postponed not only through its omission from this ten-note segment of the cycle of fifths but also through the truncation of the earlier entry of the same transposition at No. 7.

Thus the diatonic/tonal non-symmetrical component of the Intro-

[14]We could, of course, have gone on a "fishing expedition" with Allen Forte and simply looked up these pitch-class sets in his catalog, which would immediately have provided us with a means of identifying them (4-23 and 6-33, respectively).

EXAMPLE 3.27

duction collaborates with the atonal/symmetrical in preparing the way to the transposed return of the opening bassoon solo. So, most obviously of all, does the pedal-note *b* which commences at No. 10 and continues until the entry of the bassoon solo on *cb* at No. 12. And this pedal-note itself is prepared—in the pedal on its upper neighbor, *c*, at No. 7, and the pedal on its lower neighbor, *bb*, at No. 8.

In the first movement of *Le Sacre*, tonal and atonal interpretations of the same interval, a minor third, are juxtaposed. No. 33 of Bartók's *44 Violin Duets* (ex. 3.28) juxtaposes tonal and atonal interpretations of the same perfect-4th tetrachord, which is horizontally paired with its perfect-5th transposition (ex. 3.29a) and vertically paired with its tritone transposition (ex. 3.29b). The former unfolds the Dorian scale, the latter the symmetrical octatonic scale.[15] The structure of the piece as a whole derives from the implications of these two ways tetrachords are paired. In a diatonic sense the tritone transposition represents the most remote relationship, since successive transpositions by the perfect fifth reach their halfway point in the cycle of fifths at the tritone:

d c b a / g f e d / c bb a g / f eb d c / bb ab g f / eb db c bb / ab gb f eb

In an atonal sense the tritone transposition represents the closest relationship, since a second transposition by the same interval restores the original tetrachord:

ab gb f eb / d c b a / g# f# e# d#

[15] I have already referred to the exploitation of the same scale in the music of Rimski-Korsakov, Scriabin, and Stravinsky (pp. 51f., above).

33.
SONG OF THE HARVEST

U.S.Bk.No.96

EXAMPLE 3.28   Bartók, *44 Violin Duets*

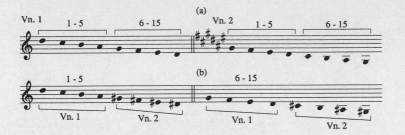

EXAMPLE 3.29

EXAMPLE 3.30

In the recapitulation (bars 21–33) the order of the two themes is reversed. The *più mosso* is a strict canon at the tritone. When it returns at bar 21 the entries of the two voices are reversed and their temporal distance narrowed, and the whole is transposed up by a semitone. This transposition of the second theme puts it in the "key" of the first theme, by simply interchanging the two tetrachords of bars 1–5 (ex. 3.30a). The conflict between the diminished-octave span of the octatonic scale and the perfect-octave span of the Dorian scale is resolved only in the last four bars. The first violin continues in the same tetrachord, and the second violin moves down by a half step. Thus the tritone that separates the two tetrachords is replaced by the perfect fifth, so that, for the first time, the two voices together unfold the Dorian octave (ex. 3.30b). The a♭ to a♮ span of bars 21–29 resolves to the a♭ to a♭ span of the same scale that the second violin unfolded alone in the first fifteen bars.

EXAMPLE 3.31

Since the octatonic scale unfolds two interval-3 cycles, transpositions of that scale by a minor third simply permute its content. Though the intervening third section of the piece, bars 16–20, returns to Tempo I in a literal inversion of the first five bars, it does so at a pitch level (ex. 3.31) that duplicates the octatonic pitch-class content of the expository statement of the second theme, bars 6–15.

In the last chapter of *Twelve-Tone Tonality*, I distinguish between the major/minor tonal system and atonality in terms of the extent to which they may be respectively defined by explicit precompositional relations, and I point to a similar distinction that has been made in the field of literary criticism:

In the traditional tonal system every simultaneity and every progression is referable to a single type of chord structure, the triad, and to the complex of functional relations postulated in the concept of a "key center." There are no precompositional principles that comparably regulate simultaneity and progression in atonal music. "The 'rightness' of a particular note depends not upon its possible containment within a pre-established harmonic unit, as it does in tonality, but upon larger compositional factors whose meaning must be discovered within the work itself."[16] The term "reflexive reference" has been suggested to describe an analogous situation in modern poetry: "Since the primary reference of any word-group

[16]Perle, *Serial Composition and Atonality*, p. 9.

is to something within the poem itself, language in modern poetry is really reflexive: the meaning-relationship is completed only by the simultaneous perception in space of word-groups which, when read consecutively in time, have no comprehensible relation to each other. Instead of the instinctive and immediate reference of words and word-groups to the objects or events they symbolize, and the construction of meaning from the sequence of these references, modern poetry asks its readers to suspend the process of individual reference temporarily until the entire pattern of internal references can be apprehended as a unity. This explanation, of course, is the extreme statement of an ideal condition rather than of an actually existing state of affairs; but the conception of poetic form that runs through Mallarmé to Pound and Eliot and which has left its traces on a whole generation of modern poets, can be formulated only in terms of the principle of reflexive reference."[17]

As in modern poetry, reflexive reference is entirely relevant and sufficient only as an explanation of an ideal, rather than an actual, musical condition. The existence of something that we identify as the "Tristan chord" suggests that in tonal music, too, it sometimes happens that "the primary reference of [a given chord] is to something inside the [composition] itself"; in atonal music, on the other hand, there may be normative and precompositional, as well as reflexively referential, elements.[18]

We have shown how within the self-referential context of Schoenberg's Opus 11, No. 1 a "window of order" emerges in the form of an explicit precompositional, or non-reflexive, element, the whole-tone collection. The "pattern of internal references" is far less reflex-

[17]Joseph Frank, "Spatial Form in Modern Literature," in *Criticism: The Foundations of Literary Judgment*, ed. Mark Schorer et al. (New York: Harcourt, Brace and World, 1958), p. 383.
[18]Perle, *Twelve-Tone Tonality*, p. 162.

EXAMPLE 3.32   Berg, Op. 3

EXAMPLE 3.33   Chopin, Prelude in E♭

ive in *Density 21.5* than it is in Opus 11, No. 1. Another cyclic partition of the twelve-tone scale, the diminished-7th chord, is the basis of the overall formal structure of the former, and this same chord engenders exactly the same formal structure in the very different harmonic and textural context of a work composed almost a quarter of a century earlier, the first movement of Stravinsky's *Le Sacre du printemps*.

A connection with *Density 21.5* which, from another point of view, is even more comprehensive is telescoped into the first two bars of an earlier work, Alban Berg's String Quartet, Opus 3 (ex. 3.32). The descending octave span of the whole, *f-f*, is symmetrically subdivided by the tritone, *b*, the final note of the head-motive. The head-motive itself—the principal melodic figure of the work—unfolds the whole-tone partitioning of the initial statement of the tritone, *f-b*, elaborated by the double-neighbor ornament of its final note. The span from this note to the lower *f* presents the alternative minor-3rd partitioning of the tritone. This initial presentation of the head-motive and its enclosing octave is a summation, in reversed order, of the structural basis of *Density 21.5*, the alternative symmetrical partitionings of the tritone. The crucial role of the interval cycles throughout this first entirely atonal composition of Berg's is foreshadowed in the opening gesture of this early work.

To look for a series of direct "influences" from one composer to the next as an explanation for these connections between Berg, Stravinsky, and Varèse is obviously fatuous and is impossible to support on historical grounds. If such connections are to be explained by "influences," it is the common influence on all of them of the twelve-tone scale, the cyclic/symmetrical structure of which suggests corresponding cyclic/symmetrical structures derivable from the interval numbers that are factors of 12. Thus in the most natural way, the differentiating partitions of the universal pitch-class set emerge: the whole-tone scale, the diminished-7th chord, the augmented triad, the tritone; and within these we have further differentiating partitions—the whole-tone scale into the augmented triad and the tritone, the diminished-7th chord into the tritone. And though the qualitative transformation in the language of music that is implied in all this manifested itself rather suddenly, within a few years in the early part of this century, that transformation has a long prehistory in the tonal progressions that symmetrically partition the octave in the music of Schubert and Chopin and Liszt and Wagner. I conclude this chapter with the even more radical example of a cyclic progression in Chopin that brings my book on *Twelve-Tone Tonality* to a close (ex. 3.33).[19]

[19]I am indebted to Mark DeVoto for calling this passage to my attention.

LECTURE IV Pitches or Pitch-Classes?

The earliest special study that we have on rhythmic procedures in the music of Alban Berg is a very valuable and probing article by Wolfgang Stroh.[1] It identifies the series of notes shown in Example 4.1 as the tone row of the third movement of the *Lyric Suite*. The example shows the row as a series of pitch classes, devoid of all implication respecting contour and rhythm. The notes as given in Stroh's example would better have been represented by pitch-class names, *f-e-c*, etc., or pitch-class numbers, 5-4-0, etc. But there is nothing in the way Berg exploits this tone row to justify such an abstract representation. Stroh demonstrates what he calls the "constructive rhythm" (ex. 4.2) by a particular distribution of the notes that he finds at one point in the movement. It is *only* in its concrete form, as a series of registrally and rhythmically related *pitches*, not as an abstract succession of pitch classes, that Berg's row gives rise to the two segments of the rhythmic theme. Example 4.1 is *not* the tone row of the third movement of the *Lyric Suite*; Example 4.3 is its tone row. The two rhythmic motives are already implicit in this very first statement of the row. Berg has neither "derived" a rhythm from the row nor imposed an invented serial rhythm onto it. The authenticity and originality of his

[1]Wolfgang Martin Stroh, "Alban Berg's 'Constructive Rhythm,'" *Perspectives of New Music* VII/1 (Fall–Winter 1968): 26.

EXAMPLE 4.1

EXAMPLE 4.2

EXAMPLE 4.3

rhythmic genius lie precisely in this: his discovery and exploitation of a rhythm that is *already* expressed in the normal form of the row, the successive pitches of which are undifferentiated in duration and registrally distributed so as to unfold a seven-note segment of the chromatic scale—the interval-1 cycle. It is precisely this registral partitioning that is eliminated in the pitch-class reading of the row, given in Example 4.1.

In thus characterizing Stroh's misrepresentation of Berg's tone row, we admit the usefulness of the term "pitch class," which is defined as follows in the *New Grove*: "The set of all pitches that are transpositions of some given pitch by zero or an integral number of octaves. All D's, for example, are members of the pitch class D." In my second lecture I called attention to the fact that the fundamental change in the language of music in our century has given rise to a special terminology. That special terminology can help us to understand the nature of the change. Schoenberg, as a composer, understood very well that inversional complementation in his twelve-tone music was an operation affecting pitch class rather than pitch relations. Had he also understood this as a theorist he would, perhaps, have been less likely to make invalid comparisons between thematic procedures in the music of Bach and Beethoven and precompositional serial relations in his own twelve-tone music. But a mere substitution of the term "pitch class" for "pitch" or "note," as in "pitch-class set theory," is no guarantee of insightful analysis. On the contrary, it tends to encourage the sort of error that Stroh managed to make in Example 4.1 without the benefit of that term.

The terrestrial musicologist will recognize the limited relevance of a characterization of the diatonic scale as a "collection of pitch classes." He will know that it is impossible to define even the most fundamental postulates of diatonic tonality without moving beyond a mere description of the relative pitch-class content of the diatonic scale—without taking into consideration voice-leading implications. The relevance of a characterization of the twelve-tone row as a "series of pitch classes" can be equally limited. It is perhaps the general failure to move beyond this conception of the tone row that accounts more than anything else for the long-prevalent view that Berg's departures from the twelve-tone practice of Schoenberg were to be "explained" as "licenses," symptomatic of an ad hoc approach to twelve-tone composition.

Example 4.4 shows the tone row of the first movement of the *Lyric Suite*. Near the beginning of the recapitulation section there is a change of octave register, effected by transposing a four-note segment of the row through the successive degrees of the interval-3 cycle (ex. 4.5). This, too, is something that must remain unobserved or in-

EXAMPLE 4.4

EXAMPLE 4.5   Berg, *Lyric Suite*, 1st mvt.

Copyright 1927 by Universal Edition. Copyright renewed. All Rights Reserved. Used by permission of European American Music Distributors Corporation, sole U.S. and Canadian agent for Universal Edition A.G., Wien.

explicable to the analyst who concentrates all his attention on "pitch classes." The achievement of such a change of register through a sequential progression is a familiar procedure in the music of the "common practice." The significant distinction is that where Berg subdivides the registral span into equal, i.e., cyclic, intervals, his tonal predecessors subdivide it, in changing register through sequential transference, into the unequal intervals of the diatonic scale. As I pointed out in my last lecture, however, the qualitative transformation in the language of music which we have experienced in our century has a long prehistory. Beginning with Schubert, we occasionally find normal diatonic functions questioned in changes of key that progress along the intervals of the whole-tone scale, or the diminished-7th chord, or the augmented triad. An even more radical example of a cyclic progression in a tonal composition is shown in Example 4.6, from Wagner (*Die Walküre*, Act III). In my last lecture

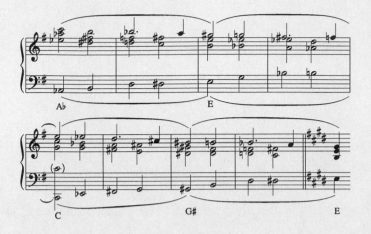

EXAMPLE 4.6   Wagner, *Die Walküre*, Act III

I showed the same continuing descent through the major third or its enharmonic equivalent in a passage from the second movement of Mahler's Ninth Symphony (ex. 3.5). But where Wagner substitutes for the descending cyclic interval the ascending complementary interval of a minor sixth or augmented fifth and smoothly fills in this enlarged space with passing chords and a diminished-7th chord on the leading-tone of the new "key," Mahler brutally emphasizes the conflict between cyclic symmetry and diatonic asymmetry by simply juxtaposing the successive major-3rd transpositions of a plain, root-position, I-V₇ figure. Example 4.7 demonstrates the essential similarity of their progression through the octave. In both, the descending major-3rd cycle in the bass unfolds simultaneously with another interval cycle in the top voice, a descending semitonal scale in the excerpt from Wagner and a descending whole-tone scale in the excerpt from Mahler.

We have seen that symmetrical partitionings in Op. 11, No. 1 and in *Density 21.5* serve to unify a series of small-scale pitch relations and to comprehend them within an overall large-scale structure. Example 4.5 demonstrates that symmetrical partitionings can also serve a

EXAMPLE 4.7(a)   Wagner

EXAMPLE 4.7(b)   Mahler

purely incidental and local function. If, in fulfilling such a traditional function as octave transference, Berg departs so radically from tradition, through his substitution of a symmetrical partitioning of the octave for the asymmetrical partitionings of the major/minor system, he departs just as radically from the twelve-tone tradition that is represented in the music of Schoenberg and Webern, for whom the twelve-tone series was *always* an integral structure that could be transposed only as a unit, and for whom twelve-tone music always implied a constant and equivalent circulation of the totality of pitch classes. Schoenberg and Webern would have asked, for each segment of the sequence in Example 4.5, where are the other eight notes of the row?

The extent to which Berg conceives of a characteristic contour as a fundamental attribute of his twelve-tone series is suggested in the

EXAMPLE 4.8

relation between the two series on which the last movement of the *Lyric Suite* is based (ex. 4.8). Through registral partitioning, the first series generates the two halves of the second. In *Lulu* the characterization of the different series by referential contours associates these with the Basic Series through shared melodic cells. Some of these ordered invariant relations are illustrated in Example 4.9. A description of such relations in terms of pitch-class ordering is not merely inadequate. It is fundamentally wrong.

Example 4.10 shows a revision of the characteristic contours of the Basic Series and of Lulu's Series for the sake of a voice-leading configuration, a whole-tone cycle commencing in the top voice and completed in the bass. Such voice-leading configurations play a pervasive role for Berg from his earliest works on, and that role persists in spite of the special constraints of the twelve-tone series. Linearity and directed motion in *Lulu* are expressed through the interval cycles, either the semitonal or perfect-5th cycles that directly unfold the twelve-tone scale, or the whole-tone, minor-3rd, major-3rd, or tritone cycles that symmetrically partition it. Example 4.10 shows a locally significant voice-leading configuration in *Lulu*. Example 4.11 shows one that unfolds over the largest dimensions of the opera, in the semitonal descent of the top voice that takes us from the final chord of Act I through the final chord of Act II to the final chord of Act III.

But if such essential aspects of this or any other music will escape the notice or comprehension of the analyst who concentrates his whole attention on pitch classes, other essential aspects will suffer the

EXAMPLE 4.9

EXAMPLE 4.10

EXAMPLE 4.11

same fate when the same exclusivity is given to pitches. The Basic Series owes its priority among the various twelve-tone series and tropes of *Lulu*, and its pervasive role in the opera, to a precompositional structure that can be defined only in terms of pitch classes. In my last lecture I proposed that diatonic collections in *Le Sacre* should be interpreted as telescoped seven-note segments of the cycle of fifths, and in support of this interpretation I called attention to "the presence of collections derived from such segments of less and more than seven degrees of the cycle." Can the cycle of fifths have any useful structural meaning for a twelve-tone collection? It can, provided we partition the latter into subsets, as Berg does in an example I cite from the *Lyric Suite*.[2] The first movement is based on three sets that are partitioned into segments which share the same pitch-class content (ex. 4.12). This shared content defines what we might call the principal "tonality" of the movement. The source of this pitch-class content is shown in the third of these sets, which is simply a hexachordal division of the cycle of fifths. The opera *Lulu* is based on a large number of different 12-tone sets. The Basic Series, at its primary

[2]Collections of all twelve pitch classes can be differentiated from one another only by assigning an order to the pitch classes or by partitioning them into mutually exclusive sub-collections. The ordering principle is the basis of the twelve-tone system formulated by Schoenberg, the partitioning principle the basis of the system formulated around the same time by Hauer. In Schoenberg's compositional practice, however, the concept of a segmental pitch-class content is represented as well, as a basis for the association of paired inversionally related set forms. On the relation between Schoenberg and Hauer see Bryan R. Simms, "Who First Composed Twelve-Tone Music, Schoenberg or Hauer?" *Journal of the Arnold Schoenberg Institute* X/2 (November 1987).

EXAMPLE 4.12

EXAMPLE 4.13

pitch level, is simply another permutation of the same segmentation of the cycle of fifths that we saw in Example 4.12c and that establishes the principal harmonic area of the first movement of the *Lyric Suite*. In *Lulu* Berg derives certain structural implications from the relation of the Basic Series to its pitch-class source that are analogous to those which we derive from the relation of the diatonic scale to the cycle of fifths in tonal music. All four forms of the set in Example 4.13 have the same hexachordal content, but the order of these segments, as defined by content only, is reversed in the second pair. Transposition by

EXAMPLE 4.14

EXAMPLE 4.15

a perfect fifth will revise the pitch-class content of each hexachord through the replacement of a single element of the hexachord by its tritone. Thus the transposition of P_0 to the fifth above in Example 4.14 only interchanges B and F between the two hexachords, and its transposition to the fifth below only interchanges B♭ and E. The hexachordal pitch-class structure of the Basic Series in *Lulu* plays an essential role in establishing referential pitch levels and differentiated harmonic areas.

The Circus Music that commences at bar 9 of the Prologue immediately demonstrates the dependence of the Basic Series on a pervasive harmonic texture to which the sets themselves are subordinate. The initial chord (ex. 4.15a) combines several salient musical elements of the opera (ex. 4.15b): the initial triadic segments of Alwa's Series and of the prime and inverted forms of the Basic Series, and the invariant tetrachord shared by the prime and inverted forms of one

EXAMPLE 4.16

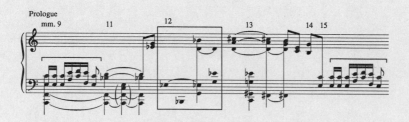

EXAMPLE 4.17

of the chief Basic Cells. Example 4.15a is a symmetrical tetrachord, which is to say that it may be bisected into pairs of equivalent intervals (in the present instance, two major thirds separated by a perfect fourth, or two perfect fourths separated by a major third) or a pair of symmetrically related but non-identical intervals. The composer exploits the major-3rd division to progress through the first four and last four components of a closed cycle of perfect-4th transpositions of the initial chord (ex. 4.16). This progression provides the background structure of the Circus Music (Prologue, bars 9–16) (ex. 4.17). The linkage of adjacent chords through overlapping major thirds is interrupted between the fourth and fifth chords, which are tritone-related, and therefore symmetrically related as well (ex. 4.16). Here again one can see a possible analogy with tonal music, where one might move away from the tonic in the direction of the dominant and subsequently, via a more esoteric relation, return to the tonic from the direction of the sub-dominant.

An analysis of the Circus Music in terms only of pitch, rather than pitch-class relations, would miss the mark entirely. So would a pitch-class analysis that merely showed how every note in this episode can be traced to one or another 12-tone row, as, indeed, it can be. A comprehensive analysis of this music must commence with recognition of the extent to which its language derives from precompositional pitch-class relations that it shares with other music, and though these pitch-class relations are still far from providing a normative background structure, analogous to what we were once accustomed to in the music of the major/minor system, they seem to take a large and most interesting step in that direction. Which is not to suggest that we should be indifferent to the component of "reflexive reference" in this music. I can think of no more appropriate elucidation of this point than the wise concluding words of Paul Lansky's article on "Pitch-Class Consciousness":

> I hope it is clear from the preceding discussion that the ways in which pitches represent pitch classes, and the ways pitch classes abstract pitch, must be *examined* in order to describe *any* kind of musical sense or progression, and that if one steps back into abstracted considerations derived without respect to such concerns, an understanding of the qualities of musical uniqueness will continue to be suppressed in favor of generalizations, which at best evoke a vague sense of what a piece may be doing, perhaps in common with some other pieces, but not what one piece *is* doing, all by itself.[3]

That different atonal pieces may be doing something "in common," and not at all in "a vague sense" but in the same precise and positive sense in which we showed Wagner and Mahler to be doing something

---

[3]Paul Lansky, "Pitch-Class Consciousness," *Perspectives of New Music* XIII/2 (Spring–Summer 1975): 65.

EXAMPLE 4.18

EXAMPLE 4.19

in common, remains a fact of uncommon interest. The value of the analysis to which we subjected *Density 21.5* in Lecture 3 was demonstrated in the insights thereby gained into another piece whose surface features are very different, the Introduction to *Le Sacre du printemps*.

But is there not more to be said about *Density 21.5* "all by itself"? So far I have made no reference whatever to the first note of the composition, either as pitch class or as pitch, in spite of its obvious importance as the initial element of what is clearly the principal motive of the piece (ex. 4.18). But surely only a Martian musicologist would take issue with an interpretation of Example 4.19 which, since it was concerned only with the tonality of the piece, made no mention of the recurrent *eb* but simply identified the rising interval of a minor sixth as deriving from the tonic triad of G minor? If I have ignored the first note of *Density 21.5*, it is not because I regard that note as unimportant but because I regard it as a component of the foreground, which has not been the focus of my analysis up to this point. Its negligible role in the background structure of bars 1–10 was implied in its omission from my sketch of that structure, which in Example 4.20 is revised to include this note.

Four levels of structural significance are represented in the exam-

EXAMPLE 4.20

ple. The octave and its subdividing tritone, *c#-g-db*, represent the first level. Within this primary tritone division, *e* and *bb* occur as passing notes that may themselves be reinterpreted as encompassing a structural tritone in which *g* would function as a passing note. The combined structural levels result in a series of minor thirds which are filled in with a second order of passing notes, *f#*, *a*, and *c*; the resulting major second between *e* and *f#* is filled in with a third order of passing note, *f*. It is its position within the interval from *e* to *g* that defines *f* as a passing note, in spite of its temporal precedence in the opening motive. This motive, the primary foreground element of the work, derives from the least significant structural level, the filled-in major second. The cyclic formation on which the whole piece, with the exception of the last five-and-a-half bars, is based is the diminished-7th chord—but neither of the intervallic components of the latter, the minor third and the tritone, is represented in the motive, as one or both would necessarily be in any motive of more than three pitch classes. Thus each of the three pitch components of the motive is a member of a *different* one of the three diminished-7th chords, and the motive *in itself* is therefore altogether uncommitted in respect to which of these partitions is structurally operative at the moment. It is only through the compositional context in which the motive occurs that we can discover which of its pitch components functions as the structural note in a given instance.

The motive, as defined in its initial statement and the repetition of this in bar 3, is characterized by its relative pitch content (a three-note segment of the semitonal scale), by its interval order—down a half

EXAMPLE 4.21

step and up a whole step—and by its rhythm (two sixteenth-notes on the beat followed by a tied eighth-note). This definitive version of the motive, combining all three attributes, occurs at only three points (not counting the repetition in bar 3), each initiating a new and major formal subdivision of the piece. As I pointed out earlier, the work falls into two parts of approximately equal length. The midpoint of each of these primary divisions is marked by a return to the definitive form of the initial motive (ex. 4.21). And the transpositional relations of these three definitive statements of the motive reflect the structure of the motive itself: the initial statement commences on *f*, the second statement on *e*, and the final statement on *f♯*.

The first major formal subdivision encompasses bars 1–14 and unfolds the principal interval-3 partition (ex. 4.20), $C3_1$ (i.e., the diminished-7th chord beginning on *c♯*). The second subdivision, encompassing bars 15–28, falls into three sections. Bars 15–17 confirm the return to the "tonic" partition in the last two notes (bars 13–14) of the first section. Bars 18–23 move into a new interval-3 partition, $C3_2$, but this remains incomplete, in that pitch-class *b* acquires its tritone associate, *f*, only in the last two notes of the composition, and there only in the context of the C2 rather than the C3 interval cycle. And bars 24–28 antiphonally unfold segments of the two partitions of C3 that have been represented to this point, $C3_1$ and $C3_2$, but in its very last note this closing section of the first half of the piece modulates, via *e♭*, to the remaining partition, $C3_0$. The latter unfolds through the third major formal subdivision (bars 29–40), which commences with a sudden and dramatic return to the climactic *g* of bar 17, and to the context of that climactic *g* in its resumption of the three-note figure, *e♯-f♯-g*, of which it is a component. The three pitch classes together give us the relative pitch-class content of the motive but none of its other attributes, though the two thirty-second-notes of the figure in bars 29–30 suggest a variant of its rhythmic attribute. The fourth and final major formal subdivision commences at bar 41 with a return to the pitch-class content of bars 29–30, but this time as an attribute of the final definitive statement of the motive. Bars 41–45 bring a return to $C3_1$, the "home key." There is a final recapitulation of $C3_1$ in bars 53–56, and then the transfiguring epilogue based on the whole-tone, or C2, partitions.

If we now reconsider the three definitive statements of the motive (ex. 4.21) we see that each occurs in the context of the "tonic" partition of the structural interval cycle. Since each note of the motive belongs to a different one of the three partitions, only one of its notes can be a member of the "tonic" partition, $C3_1$. In the initial statement (bars 1 and 3), the structural note is the second one; in the next statement (bar 15) it is the first note; and in the last statement (bar 40) it is the third. This variable relation of the basic motive of *Density 21.5* to the harmonic structure of the piece, and its function in articulating and clarifying the formal design, are exactly what we would expect and take for granted in the relation between motive and background in traditional tonal music.

The motive is associated with two all-encompassing aspects of the work, the filling-in of the structural minor third and the change from one C3 partition to another. Thus one of the attributes of the motive, its relative pitch content, recurs throughout, forming variant versions of the motive. Bars 9–11 (ex. 4.22), which I discussed in some detail in my first lecture, commence with a variant that preserves only the rhythmic attribute of the motive and concludes with one that pre-

EXAMPLE 4.22   Varèse, *Density 21.5*

© *Copyright 1946 by G. Ricordi & C. SpA, Milano; Copyright Renewed. Reprinted by permission of Hendon Music, Inc., a Boosey & Hawkes Company, Sole Agent. Reprinted by permission.*

EXAMPLE 4.23

serves only its other two attributes, relative pitch content and order. The example as a whole can be seen as a statement of the motive in augmentation. In bars 20–21 and 23 (ex. 4.23) pitch- and order-defined variants of the motive, the second of these in inversion, are given special emphasis through their registral placement. At the beginning of the second half of the piece (bars 29ff.) a pitch-defined variant is embellished through reiteration and octave displacement, and at the major formal division within this section (bars 41ff.) the same pitch-class collection returns, radically reduced in range and dynamic level but still embellished through reiteration.

What utterly elementary and trivial statements we would be limited to if we tried to discuss *Density 21.5* in terms of pitch-class relations alone! We cannot even describe its background structure, the generation of the C3 cycle through the bisection of the tritone by a passing note, without moving from the notion of pitch class to that of pitch. Pitch-class terminology is even more problematical when employed in reference to successions of symmetrically related chords such as we regularly find in the music of Bartók and Berg.

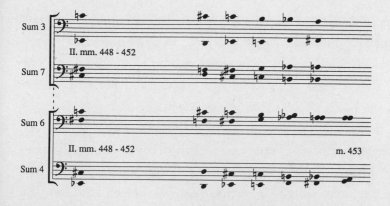

EXAMPLE 4.24

In Example 4.24, from *Lulu*, only the first chord is derived from
the tone row. The remainder are symmetrical projections of this
chord, achieved by partitioning it into a pair of dyads and maintaining the axis of symmetry of each dyad in the chords that follow. That
axis of symmetry may be identified by the sum of the two pitch-class
numbers of the dyad, with *c* represented by 0, *c#* by 1, and so on. The
first brace in the example shows the division of the initial chord into
dyads of sums 3 and 7. Through semitonal inflection each dyad progresses into another of the same sum, to form in conjunction with its
companion dyad a new chord symmetrically derived from the preceding chord. The second brace shows an alternative interpretation
of the initial chord, into dyadic sums 6 and 4. The five chords that
follow are the same as those given in the first brace, with each chord
partitioned to show the symmetrical relations defined by the alternative interpretation. In progressing from the last of these five
chords, however, the composer inflects only the sum-4 dyad, and
thus arrives at a chord that is unlike the others in the array in that it
allows of no alternative interpretation.

Of these symmetrically related chords the second doubles the *d*, the next-to-last doubles the *a*, and the last triples the *a*. I nevertheless classify them all as tetrachords, since it is obvious that there is a one-to-one correspondence between each chord and the next. The two *d*'s of the second chord must be counted as two pitches rather than as one pitch class, the two *a*'s of the sixth chord as two instances of the same pitch, and the octave and unison *a*'s of the last chord as comprising three elements, not one. There is perhaps nothing that would demonstrate the ludicrous uselessness of Allen Forte's catalog of "Prime Forms and Vectors of Pitch-Class Sets"—the whole basis of his system of analysis—so well as an attempt to locate therein such one-to-one symmetrically derived pitch collections as the second, sixth, and seventh chords of Example 4.24. For Forte and his disciples the last chord of Example 4.24 can never be anything but a dyad. It consists of two pitch classes, and that's all there is to it. There is no possible way to explain its membership in the series of chords in Example 4.24.

The voice-leading relations between the parts in Example 4.24 likewise imply pitch rather than pitch class. The voices paired on each staff move equivalent distances in opposite directions, and each voice on one staff moves equivalent distances in parallel motion with one voice on the other staff of the same brace. But this literal unfolding of the symmetrical pattern may also be interpreted as a background structure relative to which octave displacements can occur in the foreground. The thematic series of the first movement of the *Lyric Suite* (ex. 4.25a) unfolds six symmetrically related dyads, but each of these is thus related by pitch to only one other dyad (these are beamed together in the example) and by pitch class to the others. Example 4.25b shows a hypothetical version of the same series, in which literal pitch symmetry is maintained throughout, as it is in Example 4.24.

The earliest extended work by Berg, or very likely by any composer, in which symmetrical pitch relations play a consistent and sig-

EXAMPLE 4.25

EXAMPLE 4.26 Berg, Op. 3, 2nd mvt.

nificant role is the Quartet, Opus 3, composed in 1910, when Berg was only 25 (ex. 4.26). Symmetrically related dyads of sum 8 unfold both by pitch class and by pitch in the opening bars of the second movement. A most extraordinary example of octave-displaced symmetry occurs at the first entrance of viola and cello in the first movement (ex. 4.27). Their sum-1 dyad, *f-ab*, is harmonically inverted into *ab-e♯* at the beginning of bar 4, and in this version is symmetrically related by pitch to the sum-1 dyads in this and the preceding bar (*g-*

EXAMPLE 4.27   Berg, Op. 3, 1st mvt.

f# and *a-e*). The initial sum-1 dyad, *f-ab*, however, is octave-displaced in its symmetrical relation to these other sum-1 dyads—i.e., it is symmetrically related to them by pitch class rather than by pitch. The gap between the first two sum-1 dyads, *f-ab* and *g-f#*, is filled in symmetrically, the *ab* moving through *g* to *f#* and the *f* through *c* to *g*.

The application of the concepts of pitch and pitch class to the symmetrical array is complex and ambiguous, in very much the same way as it is to the diatonic scale. The characterization of the diatonic scale as a collection of pitch classes is, like the pitch-class interpretation of the symmetrical array, only partially pertinent. The voice-leading implications of both can be defined only in terms of pitch.

In my second lecture I mentioned a new musical entity which Webern was supposed to have invented: the *pensato*, a note which was to be imagined, not played. No composer has ever been more concrete, explicit, detailed, and subtle in his notation and his demands upon the performer. If Webern ever resorted to the *pensato* it could only have been because the range and precision of nuance that he required exceeded the capacity not only of his interpreters but of their instruments as well. The *pensato* would certainly have been a pitch, not a pitch class; it would have been a "real" note that the performer (and/

or the listener) would have been required to think of, with all the attributes that give a note actuality: pitch, duration, mode of attack and release, timbre, intensity.

Perhaps no one has been so influential in extending concepts and techniques originally derived from the work of Schoenberg and Webern as Milton Babbitt. In an interesting talk on Babbitt's *Sextets* for violin and piano, Joseph Dubiel argued that "the tendency of analysts to identify Babbitt pieces with their underlying twelve-tone arrays amounts to a preoccupation with compositional procedure, sometimes at the expense of auditory construal." In asking "whether it is desirable to interpret all aspects of the music as realizing the twelve-tone structure" he makes it clear that he is motivated "by appreciation for Babbitt's music" as well as "by discomfort with the literature about it." Dubiel's paper "is concerned with the relevance to perception of the twelve-tone arrays employed in the composition of Babbitt's music and routinely invoked in the analysis of it," which is to say that it is concerned with the relevance of explications of the work in terms of the pitch–class relations defined in the composition's twelve-tone array, and only there. Dubiel finds that "no particular distinction can be heard between some aspects of the surface provided for in the array and others, of the same order, less deeply grounded."[4]

I think that in thus concentrating on questions of pitch and pitch class Dubiel is overlooking another aspect of the work that is even more relevant to its "auditory construal," an oversight comparable to that of Stroh's failure to note the significance of contour in Berg's presentation of the tone row in the third movement of the *Lyric Suite*. Dubiel's criticism is limited to the pitch surface provided by the ar-

---

[4]Joseph Dubiel, " 'Thick Array / Of Depth Immeasurable': Some Questions about the Music of Milton Babbitt," a paper presented at the Fourth Michigan Conference on Music Theory, at the University of Michigan, Ann Arbor, March 29, 1985.

rays. I think it should be extended to the dynamic surface as well. Nowhere does Dubiel question Babbitt's use of twelve different levels of dynamic articulation—*ppppp, pppp, ppp, pp, p, mp, mf, f, ff, fff, ffff, fffff*— a division which seems to imply that dynamic differentiation can be in some way analogous to or in some way equated with pitch-class differentiation. Even assuming that the performers are capable of realizing and the listener of apprehending such an extended, precise, and refined scale of dynamic values, can a given dynamic value be judged independently of mode of attack, timbre, texture, register, and its relation to adjacent dynamic values? It seems to me that the explicit and absolute differentiation of twelve different dynamic levels which this music, to judge from the score, requires is based on an untenable analogy with pitch-class differentiation—most obviously untenable because, unlike the latter, it is beyond the range of "auditory construal," but for other obvious reasons as well. The pitch scale, for example, is cyclical: the interval between pitch numbers 11 and 0 is the same as that between 0 and 1. The dynamic scale is not cyclical: the interval between *fffff* and *ppppp* is not the same as that between *ppppp* and *pppp*.

But if we are nevertheless going to demand the explicit and absolute differentiation of twelve discrete dynamic levels, then we have also to establish some rules to determine the meaning of these distinctions relative to other parameters. Is the *p* in the violin on the last note of bar 7 (ex. 4.28) supposed to register the same intensity level in decibels as the *p* in the piano on the last note of bar 3, or is it only supposed to "sound"—relative to the respective differences between these two notes—*as though* it is of the same dynamic level? In the former case we establish a situation that is chaotic relative to our subjective apprehension of the required distinctions; in the second we derive our distinctions from subjective reactions that cannot possibly provide a basis for the refined differentiations that this music calls for.

EXAMPLE 4.28   Babbitt, *Sextets*

Copyright 1975 by C. F. Peters Corporation. 373 Park Avenue South, New York, N.Y. 10016.
International Copyright Secured. All Rights Reserved. Alle Rechte Vorbehalten. Used by permission.

The familiar and perhaps insoluble problem that faces every orchestral composer and every conductor—in view of the multiplicity of implications of any given dynamic marking in the context of a multiplicity of different types of instruments and a multiplicity of relations among them—of how to mark dynamic values and how to interpret these markings in correspondence with the composer's intentions is infinitely magnified in Babbitt's *Sextets*, and this in a mere duo for violin and piano.

The "auditory construal" of the rhythmic aspect of this music, which is also entirely ignored in Dubiel's paper, seems to me equally problematical. Here again an untenable analogy with pitch-class differentiation is implied in the exploitation of twelve different rhythmic elements, each defined by a different time point (a different thirty-second-note point) in the bar in an unchanging meter of 3/8. In bars 2–3 in the piano, a series of eight dynamic markings, *mp-f-pp-ppp-ff-ffff-fffff-fff*, is conjoined to eight time points (we count the first thirty-second-note in the bar as no. 0): 3, 4, 5, 6, 7, 8, 9, 10. In bars 5–7 the same conjunction of dynamic values and time points is repeated. One might expect, or hope, that such a co-ordinated repetition would be audibly, or at least visibly, identifiable as such, in spite of the association of different pitches with the second statement. I, however, can only discern this ordered succession of co-ordinated dynamic markings and time points through an analytical scrutiny of the first seven bars that has nothing to do with my intuitive response to them either as a listener or as a score reader. Time points 3, 4, 5, 6 occur in bar 2 and time points 7, 8, 9, 10 in bar 3. We know this only because we see a time signature of 3/8 and barlines, in relation to which we can partition each bar into 12 equal parts and count off the points of attack. There is no particular reason, however, for the listener who is not simultaneously perusing the score to construe a triple meter, even after repeated hearings.[5] There is nothing to mark time point 0 in bars 2 and 3, and sans score one might be more likely to construe time points 3, 4, 5, 6 and 7, 8, 9, 10 as occupying parallel positions—as time points 15, 0, 1, 2—in successive 4/8 bars (ex. 4.29). Regular readers of *Perspectives of New Music* would know better, of course, and would realize that a meter of 4/8 would imply a division by triplets. It is more difficult to hypothesize alternative construals of the repe-

[5]Cf. Joel Lester, "Notated and Heard Meter," *Perspectives of New Music* XXIV/2 (Spring–Summer 1986).

EXAMPLE 4.29

tition in bars 5–7 (ex. 4.28) of the ordered succession of co-ordinated dynamic markings and time points. Here we find time point 3 in bar 5, time point 4 in bar 6, and time points 5 through 10 packed together into bar 7.

Preliminary to his discussion of its relation to the pitch-class array, Dubiel presents a vivid description of the music. In his following remarks he takes us through bars 1–8 in the violin part and 1–5 in the piano (ex. 4.28): "The violin's opening line is exaggeratedly discontinuous: all its intervals are huge leaps, and there are drastic dynamic changes—in particular sudden stabs of forte with the upward leaps. The discontinuity is intensified by the impression that the violin line is ejected one note at a time from the piano. But toward the end of the line the violin becomes more continuous, in just these respects; it stops leaping, stays soft, and connects several notes legato." Dubiel makes no mention at all of pitch or pitch class, but he does so subsequently in very specific terms, in an analysis which leads him to his conclusion that the pitch-class array is problematical in its relevance to the voice-leading relations and pitch associations deducible from the music itself. He is not very specific as to rhythm and dynamics, either, and, regrettably, he makes no effort at all to relate these dimensions of the piece to any precompositional assumptions. An elucidation of the latter, comparable to his elucidation of the concept and function of pitch-class arrays, would have been very welcome and should really have been undertaken as part of the task he had chosen for himself.

Dubiel suggests that "we would falsify the music if our analysis didn't let it seem aggressively dazzling in tone—almost too fast to grasp." Certainly, a more precise evaluation of these non-pitch components would have contributed to the vividness of his description of the music. It is not just "sudden stabs of forte" that the violin gives us "with its upward leaps." The first "sudden stab" is to a *ff* which decays to *ppppp*, the second to a *f* which decays to *pp*, and the low note on which the violin is poised in preparation for each leap maintains, in contrast, a steady dynamic level. And however problematical of execution and apprehension, the lightning changes from one to another of the whole range of dynamic levels do produce their dazzling effect, particularly if we persevere in reading all these changes in pitch and dynamics against the indicated steady 3/8 meter, rather than falling into the line of least resistance of the mere listener, thoughtlessly and naïvely content to accept such more banal and certainly less dazzling interpretations as we illustrated in Example 4.29.

EXAMPLE 4.30   Berg, *Lyric Suite*, 6th mvt.

It should not need to be stressed that the analysis of a piece of music ought to be relevant to its perception. Even though John Cage's compositional procedures in some of his music depend on the *I Ching*, the Chinese *Book of Changes*, I would not regard it as appropriate to invoke the latter in explication of the perceived surface relations of that music. And just as surely, whatever the role of Babbitt's pitch-class arrays in his compositional procedures, to the extent that Dubiel has uncovered voice-leading connections and pitch associations that seem to be irrelevant, or problematically relevant, to these arrays, his point that it is not enough to invoke the latter in explication of the however-perceived surface relations of Babbitt's music is well taken.

Berg was the earliest composer to conceive of a special, twelve-tone, rhythmic series, in the third movement of the *Lyric Suite*, and he may also have been the first to employ, in the last bar of that same composition, a verifiable *pensato* (ex. 4.30): "The instruments drop out one by one, the four parts converging into a single line that continues into an *ostinato* on the last two notes of the derived series [ex. 4.8] and becomes inaudible on the penultimate note of the series, seemingly continuing into the silence beyond."[6]

[6]Perle, *The Operas of Alban Berg.* Vol. 2: *Lulu*, p. 14.

Composing with Symmetries

In my first lecture I referred to the futility of my attempts to deduce the principles of Schoenberg's twelve-tone system from my analytical observations of Berg's *Lyric Suite*. Other commentators on this music came to it with a disadvantage that I didn't have—they already knew something about the basic axioms of Schoenberg's system. The prefatory notes in the score, by Berg's friend and fellow Schoenberg-pupil, Erwin Stein, which must surely have had the composer's approval, present a fairly extensive overview of the formal design of the work, but as to its twelve-tone aspects we are given only a summary statement: "The work (Ist and VIth part, the main part of the IIIrd and the middle section of the Vth) has been mostly written strictly in accordance with Schoenberg's technique of the 'Composition with 12 inwardly related tones.' A set of 12 different tones gives the rough material of the composition, and the portions which have been treated more freely still adhere more or less to this technique." A memorial volume by Willi Reich, with contributions by Adorno and Krenek, was published in 1937,[1] the same year in which I came upon the score of the *Lyric Suite* for the first time. I had no opportunity to see Reich's book until some time later, but in any case the article by Adorno would have been of no help. Of the first movement, for ex-

[1]Reich, *Alban Berg*.

ample, we are told only that it is based on a twelve-tone theme, and the initial statement of this theme in the first violin is quoted. There is nothing else until ten years later, when René Leibowitz's book appeared.[2] Here are the two sentences that he devotes to the first movement: "Entirely written in the twelve-tone technique, [it] is a sonata movement without development. Thus the recapitulation follows directly upon the exposition; but, because of the highly advanced twelve-tone technique of variation, *everything* in this movement is developmental."[3] There is not a single illustration, not even of the tone row that is supposed to be the basis for "*everything* in this movement."

Faced with a striking lack of correspondence between the formulated principles of Schoenberg's technique and Berg's music, the specialists refrained from further comment on this music until another ten years had passed, when H. F. Redlich's book appeared. Redlich took the bold step of attempting an analysis in accordance with the authoritative assertions about it. Here is his description of the relation between what he calls the "Basic Set" and the initial bar (cf. pp. 7f., above): "The first movement of the *Lyric Suite* develops out of the disorder of intervals in its first bar, the notes of which, strung out horizontally, present the complete chromatic scale, and from this in the second and following bars, grows the Basic Set in its thematic shape [ex. 5.1]." The series of whole notes marked "X" in Redlich's example unfolds the four introductory chords, with the first three read in ascending order from the bass and the last in a more haphazard sequence. We are shown that all twelve pitch classes (the numbered series marked "Y") are comprised in these four chords. The numbers above the notes in the "X" series show their order position in the

[2]René Leibowitz, *Schoenberg et son école* (Paris: Janin, 1947).
[3]René Leibowitz, *Schoenberg and His School*, trans. Dika Newlin (New York: Philosophical Library, 1949), p. 157.

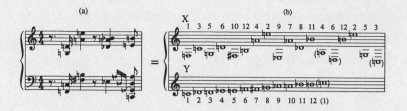

EXAMPLE 5.1   Berg, *Lyric Suite*

"Basic Set" (cf. ex. 4.12b). Redlich continues: "The function of the first bar of the *Lyric Suite*, to serve as source for the dodecaphonic development of the rest of the movement, becomes evident here."[4]

Redlich could be very perceptive indeed when it came to the expressive content of the *Lyric Suite*. I was in constant correspondence with him from 1959 until his death in 1968. He became my intimate friend in 1966–1967, when I was living in England, and his papers and correspondence relating to his 1957 book on Berg were given to me by his widow after his death. They confirm that he can have had no knowledge of a secret setting of a Baudelaire text in the finale of the *Lyric Suite*, which the American musicologist Douglass M. Green deciphered in the summer of 1976 from Berg's cryptic notations in a manuscript draft in the National Library in Vienna, and which I found a few months later, carefully and completely written out, in an annotated copy of the published score that the composer had prepared for the woman to whom he had secretly dedicated the work.[5] Yet in

[4]H. F. Redlich, *Alban Berg, the Man and His Music* (London: John Calder, 1957), pp. 135f.

[5]Douglass M. Green, "Berg's De Profundis: The Finale of the *Lyric Suite*," and George Perle, "The Secret Program of the *Lyric Suite*," *International Alban Berg Newsletter* 5 (June 1977). A longer version of the latter is published in *Musical Times* CXVIII/1614–1616 (August, September, October 1977).

his book Redlich refers to "the concealed vocality of the *Lyric Suite*."[6] When it came to the twelve-tone aspects of the same work, however, he can hardly be said to have contributed anything, in 1957, to what had been offered by Leibowitz in 1947, Adorno in 1937, and Stein in 1927.

When I looked at this music for the first time in the summer of 1937, the initial bar didn't strike me as being at all disordered, since I had not yet been informed, as Leibowitz and Redlich were by the time they came to write their respective books, that everything in the "strictly" dodecaphonic first movement had to be derived from a single serial ordering of the twelve notes of the chromatic scale. I immediately recognized that the first three chords unfold tetrachordal segments of a single statement of the cycle of fifths, and that at the bottom of the same page, in bars 7–9, the cello presents a linear statement, in reversed order, of a hexachordally segmented statement of the same cycle. In view of the unfolding of the same hexachordal content in the thematic row and in the scale motive (ex. 4.12), and the return to the initial tetrachordal segmentation of the perfect-5th cycle, linearly unfolded in the second violin at the beginning of the recapitulation, how could one speak of the initial bar as "disordered"? If anything is to be designated as an *Urform* here, surely it is this perfect-5th cycle, given its background role in relation to the tone row and other components of the movement.

It was through discoveries of this sort in the music of the *Lyric Suite* that I made my first connections with the work of the second Viennese school. But the assimilation of such discoveries to the point where they can be integrated into one's own compositional technique and vocabulary is something else again. It was not until August of 1938, exactly one year after my first encounter with the score of the

---

[6]Redlich, *Alban Berg, the Man and His Music*, p. 142.

Lyric Suite, that I wrote my first atonal piece, a *molto adagio* movement for string quartet, and this was more directly influenced by the first movement of Bartók's Second String Quartet. In the following year I began work on a string quartet in what I supposed was Schoenberg's twelve-tone system. By this time I had come to understand that this postulated that all the pitch relations of a given composition would be derived exclusively from a permutation of the twelve pitch classes—the "tone row"—that was devised especially for that composition, from the transpositions of this same permutation, and from their retrograded, inverted, and retrograde-inverted forms. I also assumed that one wouldn't make one's way through this array of forty-eight forms of the tone row in some helter-skelter fashion, but that for any given section of the piece a sort of "tonality" would be established, by limiting the row forms that would define the pitch relations of that section to a single, inversionally related, pair and their retrogrades.

Now this, as far as it goes, is not a bad description of Schoenberg's twelve-tone system at all. I found the principle of a single tone-row— a special intervallic series that would serve as a unifying structure for a given twelve-tone piece—congenial to what I was looking for as a composer myself. The concept that a specific prime form of the row would be paired with a specific inversion and the retrogrades of the same two forms would be similarly paired I saw as a corollary of this principle. Though this concept didn't seem to be at all consistent with Berg's practice in the *Lyric Suite*, it is consistent with Schoenberg's compositional practice in ways about which I knew nothing whatever at the time.[7] But in fact my understanding of the nature of the twelve-tone row and of how it could function as a source of pitch-class relations differed in the most radical way from Schoenberg's.

[7] Cf. Perle, *Serial Composition and Atonality*, 5th ed., pp. 96ff.

You might reasonably ask why I didn't simply get hold of some of Schoenberg's twelve-tone scores and deduce the principles of his twelve-tone system from them. For one thing, practically nothing was available for purchase, at least in Chicago, where I was living at the time. By that time Hitler had taken over Vienna, the home of Schoenberg's publisher, so this music was not available even there any longer. The first of Schoenberg's twelve-tone compositions that I was able to acquire were the first two American works, the Fourth Quartet and the Violin Concerto, and they were published only in that same year, 1939. The first person I met from whom I could borrow any of this music was Krenek, who was kind enough to lend me the Piano Piece, Opus 33a. When I moved to New York in 1946 upon my return from Japan after the war, one of the first things I did was to go to what was then the Music Branch of the New York Public Library, the 58th Street Branch, to see if I could again borrow a copy of this piece. Most of Schoenberg's scores were in the non-circulating reference collection, but Opus 33a was an exception. When I got home I discovered that the music had been cut out and that I had only the binding. (There was, of course, no such thing as "xeroxing" at the time.) I still have my scorched copy of Opus 33b. (I lent this piece to a friend; when his house caught on fire, this was the first thing he thought of rescuing.) The piece had been published by Henry Cowell in the April, 1932, issue of his *New Music* edition, a quarterly publication subsidized by subscription and specializing in "ultra-modern compositions" by American composers. Opus 33b was one of the occasional exceptions, and it was introduced by the following prefatory note: "Arnold Schoenberg has requested that we do not publish either biographical notes or musical explanations concerning his work, since both he and his musical viewpoint are well known."

In the period between the *molto adagio* and my string quartet, I spent many hours studying in the Newberry Library in Chicago, which had an excellent non-circulating collection of contemporary music. I can still recall the excitement of my first perusal of the scores of the Bartók Fifth Quartet and the Schoenberg Chamber Symphony, Opus 9, and of my first analytical insights into these works, but I have no similar recollection of any twelve-tone works of Schoenberg that I might have looked at during these sessions. I think an hour or so with the still unpublished Fourth Quartet would have made me realize that my idea of how the twelve-tone row worked was not at all the same as Schoenberg's, but I did not succeed in deducing his method, or even his tone row, from the first forty bars of the Third Quartet. The twelve-tone system as I then understood it was no easier to deduce from these forty bars, but neither could I readily see, in view of the problematic compositional implications of my own method, that they were necessarily inconsistent with it. I had, in fact, unknowingly invented my own twelve-tone system and usefully, perhaps wilfully, misconceived Schoenberg's because of my own needs as a composer and because of my own expectations for a post-diatonic musical language.

Here is the principal pair of prime and inverted forms of the row of my projected string quartet:

P: *b c d f a a♭ g f♯ d♯ e b♭ c♯*
I: *b b♭ a♭ f c♯ d d♯ e g f♯ c a*

In my first lecture I described some of the ways the twelve-tone compositional procedures that I discovered on the very first page of the *Lyric Suite* stood in opposition, though I did not know this at the time, to Schoenberg's concepts and practice. One of these was the derivation of "a second thematic version of the series . . . through the cyclical permutation of the first version." The third movement of the *Lyric Suite* goes much further in this direction. The prime form of the series is employed throughout in three different rotations. I went still further and assumed a twelve-tone system in which the row didn't function as a thematic structure at all. I made no distinction among the twelve rotations of the row. Thus for me the "first" note of the above "P" form, *b*, would be understood to have *c♯* to its left, and the "last" note, *c♯*, would be understood to have *b* to its right. Even the most cursory glance at the Fourth Quartet should have informed me that this concept was totally at odds with Schoenberg's, but, as I've said, the work was not yet published by the time I began to speculate along these lines. But I rather doubt that the availability of the score would have made any difference. I was interested in what I *wanted* the twelve-tone system to be, rather than in what it actually *was*, and I didn't ruminate over the possibility that there might be a difference between the two.

My second mistaken assumption about the twelve-tone system has no precedent whatever either in Berg's work or in Schoenberg's. By the time I began work on my first string quartet I correctly understood that "in Schoenberg's twelve-tone system all the tone relations that govern a given musical context are referable to a specific linear ordering of the twelve notes of the semitonal scale," as I put it in *Serial Composition and Atonality*.[8] But this really tells us nothing that has any compositional consequences unless we define what we mean by "referable." We have seen that Redlich, in trying to explain the introductory bar of the *Lyric Suite*, was also able to refer it to a specific linear ordering of the twelve notes of the semitonal scale, but that the terms in which he did so made it equally referable to any other one of the 479,001,600 permutations of the twelve pitch classes.

My concept of referability derived from the assumption that the pitch class to the left and the pitch class to the right of any given pitch class in the prime form of the row, and the pitch class on either side

[8]Ibid., p. 2.

of the same given pitch class in an associated inverted form, defined the closest pitch-class relations of the axial pitch class. This, in itself, is consistent enough with Schoenberg's own concept of the row. Indeed, in some brief notes that he wrote shortly before his death and that were published for the first time in 1975, he presents this point of view in the most unambiguous terms: "Every tone appears always in the neighbourhood of two other tones in an unchanging combination which produces an intimate relationship most similar to the relationship of a third and a fifth to its root. . . . If dissonances other than the catalogued ones are admitted at all in music, it seems that the way of referring them all to the basic set is the most logical and controllable procedure toward this end."[9] But I went on to assume that the four pitch classes in this "intimate relationship" to the axial pitch class formed a cluster within which the axial pitch class could move at will. Thus the *e* in the above pair of P and I forms might progress to or be combined with any or all of the notes immediately adjacent to it—*d#* and *bb* from P, and *d#* and *g* from I—and any of these "neighbor notes" might in turn be construed as "axis notes." The retrograde versions of the paired P and I forms would have no independent meaning, since they provided no new "intimate relationships." They simply implied that from any point on the row one was always free to move in either direction. But one was also free to move, via the shared axis note, to the inversionally related form of the row, and to progress to either or both of its neighbor notes there. I was not particularly concerned about the fact that the same pitch class might be represented more than once in certain neighbor-note configurations. This I saw as a specific characteristic of a particular pairing of the P and I forms. If this same pair, this same "mode," were to be transposed up by a semitone, to a new "key," we would find *f* similarly

[9]Schoenberg, *Style and Idea* (1975), pp. 246f.

conjoined with *e* and *b* from P and *e* and *g♯* from I. On the other hand, if the former were retained at its original pitch level and only the latter transposed to the higher semitone, this would give us a new "mode" and *e* would be provided with a neighbor-note configuration of four different pitch classes—*d♯* and *b♭* from the P form and *e* and *g♯* from the I form.[10]

I managed to compose fourteen bars of my string quartet before I found it impossible to proceed any further in what I still thought was *the* twelve-tone system. I liked, and still like, those fourteen bars, and expected to get back to them some day, so I called my next quartet the Second. I recently finished my Eighth String Quartet, but this should really be called the Seventh, in view of the fate of the First. On the other hand, I have two Fourth Quartets, both of them discarded, as are also the Second, Third, and Sixth.

I was still struggling with my First String Quartet when I had my first lesson with Ernst Krenek in the summer of 1939. Krenek was

[10]I said above that my "mistaken assumption" that one could move via a common tone between inversionally related set forms "has no precedent whatever either in Berg's work or in Schoenberg's." It has a precedent, however, in an article, unknown to me at the time, by the American musicologist Richard S. Hill, who, in "Schoenberg's Tone-Rows and the Tonal System of the Future," *Musical Quarterly* XXII/1 (January 1936), presented the first really comprehensive survey of Schoenberg's twelve-tone procedures. Mr. Hill anticipated my criticism of the motivic aspect of the Schoenbergian tone row and regarded the elimination of this aspect as a necessary first step in the evolution of the row into a functional mode. He suggested (p. 34) that "it should be perfectly possible to repeat the same segment . . . in sequences without having the rest of the notes occur in the other parts," exactly as Berg, who is not mentioned in the article, does in the example (4.5) from the *Lyric Suite* that I quoted above. He went on to propose "that one could proceed from any note only to one of the four notes next to it in the series—that is, to the note before and after it in the prime and mirror. . . . This would, of course, destroy the last vestige of the motival nature of the row, and in its place substitute that of the functional mode. But after all, why not? Motives are things that should vary with each piece; modes must stay fairly constant."

the first person I ever met with whom I could discuss questions of twelve-tone theory.

> I had looked him up when he was in Chicago for a performance with the Symphony during the preceding season and he had invited me to meet with him for occasional private lessons at the University of Michigan, where he was to be a guest professor during the summer session. I showed him my fourteen bars in the "twelve-tone system" at our first meeting, and was dismayed when he explained to me that in Schoenberg's twelve-tone system each element of any form of the series progressed to the next in the given form and was not regarded as intersecting with an element of the same pitch [class] in another form of the same series. I was dismayed not because I had made a "mistake"—in fact, Krenek was generous enough to call what I had come up with a "discovery"—but because Schoenberg's idea of the series seemed so primitive compared to mine. I had thought that the series must be something like a scale, functioning as the background structure of a piece, even though, unlike the diatonic scale, it was specific to that piece. The Schoenbergian series was simply a disguised ostinato twelve-tone motive. It was almost like defining the tonality of a piece in E major by simply playing the scale of E major over and over again.[11]

It did not for a moment occur to me to give up my variant of the twelve-tone system for Schoenberg's, in spite of the trouble I was having in getting beyond the fourteenth bar of my string quartet. I had already attributed my difficulties to the absence of any coherent relationship among the twelve axis- and neighbor-note combinations

---

[11]*Perle on Perle: The Composer Recalls His Life in Music*, an interview by Dennis Miller (Englewood, N.J.: Music Associates of America, 1987), p. 9.

comprised in any given pairing of P and I forms, not to speak of the 144 such combinations comprised in the twelve non-equivalent pairings, or "modes." Now that I realized that the twelve-tone system I had come up with was in any case not the same as Schoenberg's, I looked for a solution without concerning myself about antecedent concepts of the twelve-tone system.

Hitchhiking home from Ann Arbor after my first lesson with Krenek, it occurred to me that if one employed the semitonal scale or the cycle of fifths as a tone row, the 144 axis- and neighbor-note combinations and their twelve transpositions would be reduced to just one and its twelve transpositions. If, for example, in place of the P and I forms of the series of my First Quartet, we pair two semitonal scales moving in opposite directions, *e* will always have as its neighbor notes, from either form of the scale and regardless of "mode" or "key" of the paired forms, *d#* and *f*, and every other axis- and neighbor-note combination will only transpose this same collection. Any pair of inversionally related statements of the cycle of fifths will similarly give us *a* and *b* as neighbors to *e*, and only transpositions of this collection. This was obviously not a solution to the problem of the chaotic heterogeneity of neighbor-note relations of the general twelve-tone set—or, to put it another way, it was too perfect a solution.

But suppose the alternate elements of the row itself were inversionally related, as they are in the first movement of the *Lyric Suite* (ex. 5.2). Each neighbor-note pair of any form of a row derived in this way from inversionally related statements of the perfect-5th (interval-7) cycle preserves the same interval (i.e., *difference*), the perfect fifth; each axis note preserves the same axes of symmetry in relation to its neighbor notes (i.e., the same pair of *sums*), depending on the transposition of the row. The row form that generates the neighbor-note relations shown in Example 5.3 alternately unfolds

EXAMPLE 5.2

EXAMPLE 5.3

dyads of sums 1 and 6 (mod 12). We show this row form below in both letter-name and pitch-class number notation. We define the "p" aspect of the row by counting "up" from the even sum and "down" from the odd, and the "i" aspect conversely. These alternating dyadic sums will also define the pitch level of a row. Thus, for example, "p_3p_8" transposes "p_1p_6" to the semitone above. Ascending, or P, cycles are shown in boldface in these representations of what we will henceforth call "cyclic sets." If the alternative cycle were the one shown in boldface we would interpret the set as being in the interval-5 rather than the interval-7 system and would call it i_1i_6 instead of p_1p_6.

bb **eb** eb **bb** ab **f** db **c** f# **g** b **d** e **a** a **e** . . .
pitch-class nos.: 10 **3** 3 **10** 8 **5** 1 **0** 6 **7** 11 **2** 4 **9** 9 **4** . . .
sum 1: └──┘ └──┘ └──┘ └──┘ └──┘ └──┘ └──┘ └──┘
sum 6: └──┘ └──┘ └──┘ └──┘ └──┘ └──┘ └──┘

Like the thematic row of the first movement of the *Lyric Suite*, this cyclic set is symmetrical, in that its retrograde is identical to its tritone transposition. At the points of intersection of the cyclic intervals

EXAMPLE 5.4

EXAMPLE 5.5

there are pitch-class repetition and a tritone (= retrograde) restatement of the row. If we pair the prime form with an inverted form, we generate neighbor-note configurations comprising two perfect fifths, their respective pitch levels depending on the respective pitch levels of the paired forms. Let us assume that the preceding form of the interval-7 set is paired with an inversion that generates alternating sums 3 and 10:

b♭ f f b♭ c e♭ g a♭ d c♯ a f♯ e b b e . . .

The axis- and neighbor-note combinations produced by these paired forms of the interval-7 row are shown in Example 5.4.

The following pair of cyclic set-forms will produce another type of neighbor-note configuration (ex. 5.5):

p_7p_0: *g c c g f d b♭ a d♯ e g♯ b c♯ f♯ f♯ c♯* . . .
i_1i_8: *a e e a b d f♯ g d♭ c a♭ f e♭ b♭ b♭ e♭* . . .

Neighbor-note configurations comprising two semitones will be generated by rows analogously derived from inversionally related statements of the interval-1 cycle. For example, suppose we pair the interval-1 row form that alternately unfolds dyadic sums 0 and 1 with its inversion that alternately unfolds dyadic sums 8 and 7:

p_1p_0: *c♯ c c c♯ b d b♭ e♭ a e a♭ f g f♯ f♯ g* . . .
i_7i_8: *e♭ e e e♭ f d f♯ c♯ g c a♭ b a b♭ b♭ a* . . .

The axis- and neighbor-note combinations will be the same as those shown in Example 5.5. In the former instance the neighbor-note configurations are read as perfect fifths separated by a semitone; in the latter they are read as semitones separated by a perfect fifth. The respective axis note associated with each neighbor-note cluster is unchanged because the four dyadic sums are the same.

Within an hour or so after my return from my first trip to Ann Arbor I had worked out the various types and arrays of symmetrically and transpositionally related chords that could be derived in this way from the cyclic set, though I was still very far away—decades away, in fact—from being able to explain these in terms of "axes of symmetry" or "sums" and from any awareness of the general relevance of the concepts of the interval cycle and symmetry to the music of the mainstream composers of the twentieth century in general, and of Berg and Bartók in particular. I was looking for a solution to practical compositional problems of the sort that had made it impossible for me to proceed beyond the fourteenth bar of my first attempt at twelve-tone composition. But it was only after a year and a number of false starts that I was able to compose anything with these highly structured patterns, which seemed to hold so much more promise of a background level for twelve-tone music than did the "conventional" twelve-tone system. I had first of all to understand the axis- and neighbor-note collections as what I have just called them—"chords." By this time I already knew, in a way, too much about atonality and the twelve-tone system; before I could compose any-

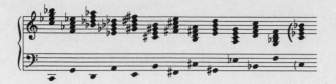

EXAMPLE 5.6

thing with these arrays, I had to find my way back to what a "chord" had meant in the major/minor system, back to the concept of a preestablished harmonic unit to which the pitch-class content of every simultaneity could be referred.

In the traditional tonal system, whatever is not definable as a triad is definable as a dissonance on its way from and to a triad. I was still a long way from understanding, or even considering, what "dissonance" might mean in my new twelve-tone system, but in my first piece in that system, composed in August of 1940, everything is definable as one or another chord in the given array. The two inversionally related row forms, based on the perfect-5th cycle, are as follows:

p_7p_0: *g   c   c   g   f   d   bb   a   d♯   e   g♯   b   c♯   f♯   f♯   c♯* . . .
i_3i_{10}: *bb   f   f   bb   c   eb   g   ab   d   c♯   a   f♯   e   b   b   e* . . .

Let us shift these relative to each other so that parallel cycles are vertically aligned to show a complete series of shared axis notes:

g   c   c   g   f   d   bb   a   d♯   e   g♯   b   c♯   f♯   f♯   c♯   b   g♯   e   d♯   a   bb   d   f (g
bb   c   eb   g   ab   d   c♯   a   f♯   e   b   b   e   f♯   a   c♯   d   ab   g   eb   c   bb   f   f (bb

In Example 5.6 cyclic and symmetrical relations generated in this alignment of the two row forms are represented in staff notation. There is no compositional interpretation, in Example 5.6, of the basic paradigmatic model of the array, but a first step in the direction of

EXAMPLE 5.7

EXAMPLE 5.8

such an interpretation is unavoidably implied in the alternation, for practical reasons, of perfect fourths and fifths in what would ideally be a series of one or the other exclusively. In Example 5.7 we take a second step in the direction of a compositional interpretation of the array, by applying the traditional voice-leading rules of elementary tonal harmony to the neighbor-note configurations. The general twelve-tone set, defined by the order of pitch classes, cannot be deduced from fewer than eleven of its elements—even after we have defined the order of ten of these, we still have implied nothing about the order of the remaining two. In fact, the tone row of the first movement of the *Lyric Suite* and the tone row of the third movement differ only in the interchange of two pitch classes (ex. 5.8). The cyclic set, however, is fully represented and fully implied by any one of its three-note segments, each of which gives us the cyclic interval and the two sums that define its symmetrical relations. We are therefore under no more constraint to progress along the cycle of fifths, in the

EXAMPLE 5.9

compositional interpretation of the above array, than we would be to progress exclusively by root progressions of the perfect fifth in the major/minor system, in spite of their hierarchical priority in the latter. In earlier examples (5.4–5.5) we showed another possible step toward a compositional interpretation of the paradigmatic model by laying out the chords along the interval-1 rather than the interval-7 cycles. We might similarly modify the paradigmatic model in Example 5.6 by partitioning it into cycles of any other interval (C2 and C6 partitions are illustrated in ex. 5.9) and go on from there to apply traditional voice-leading rather than cyclic principles in the unfolding of the neighbor-note configurations. In Example 5.10 the precompositional relations are based on shared dyads that represent the symmetrical relations of the axis note to each of its neighbors: the sum-0 and sum-7 dyads of one form of the cyclic set, and the sum-10 and sum-3 dyads of the inversionally related form. (The axis notes are shown as whole-notes in the example.)

I did not think in terms of these paradigmatic models and background structures when I composed my first piece in what I now call "twelve-tone tonality" and what I then called "the twelve-tone modal

EXAMPLE 5.10

system." These are the result of reflections, long after the fact, on the successive stages of interpretation by which that composition may be related to the original, uninterpreted, array. Nor do I think of paradigmatic models and background structures now when I compose. In my first lecture I tried to elucidate the compositional process as I understand it. I described the composer as first of all a listener, and I emphasized that the intuitive component of the listening experience is also a component of the composing experience. In this respect I don't think there is any real difference between a good composer and a good performer. Here is what a writer who specializes in such questions has to say about the listening experience: "Without any advance knowledge, without any contribution from the analytical faculty, the ear perceives both overt and hidden tonal relations, integrates and differentiates according to the given organic structure, distinguishes between superordinate and subordinate elements."[12] This is how the composer must hear what he is composing as he composes it. And here is the same writer on the composing experience: "One thing is certain: no good piece of music is ever done backwards, as it were, from the background to the foreground, beginning with the construction of some interesting abstract pattern and then filling in the music. This would be comparable to building up a living organism by finishing the skeleton first, then putting in the organs, muscles, ligaments, etc. Composing is not different from other creative intellectual activities in that it relies primarily on a spontaneous sequence of ideas."[13] This is not a plea for ignorance; it does not assert that a composer who knew nothing about the harmonic vocabulary of diatonic tonality and its system of key relations could have written Beethoven's Fifth Symphony.

The cyclic series is comparable to the diatonic scale in that it can function as a general set on which any number of pieces can be based, but it was a while before any "spontaneous sequence of ideas" that could relate in an organic way to the background structure provided by the cyclic array occurred to me. This first composition of mine in my own special version of the twelve-tone system was also the first to find a publisher. It appeared in an anthology of music by composers of the United States, published in 1941 in Montevideo as part of a special issue of the *Boletín Latino-Americano de Música*, that also contained compositions by thirty-four other composers, including Luen-

[12]Victor Zuckerkandl, *Man the Musician* (Princeton: Princeton University Press, 1973), p. 195.
[13]Victor Zuckerkandl, *The Sense of Music* (Princeton: Princeton University Press, 1959), p. 216.

EXAMPLE 5.11 Perle, Modal Suite, 1st mvt.
Copyright 1941 by Boletin latíno-americano de música, V. Used by permission.

ing, Copland, Diamond, Carter, Cowell, Riegger, Piston, Crawford, Schuman, and Ives. The last was represented by *The Unanswered Question*, which was published in this collection for the first time anywhere.

The first movement of my little suite is shown in Example 5.11. I

EXAMPLE 5.12

have bracketed the "spontaneous idea" (A) with which the first phrase commences, and corresponding segments (B, C, and D) of each of the following phrases. The composition itself might be understood as a final interpretation of the same array that we have taken through a series of precompositional interpretations in Examples 5.6–5.7 and 5.9–5.10. I trust I have made it clear that in making such a statement I am asserting nothing whatever about the conscious compositional process. I would even go further and claim it is essential that these preliminary stages of interpretation should persist at the intuitive level. It is precisely in this way, by addressing itself to the composer's inner ear, that the array fulfills its function as a background structure. This is what makes it a "background."

In the array, Example 5.11A derives from two, inversionally equivalent, axis-note chords (ex. 5.12), unfolding the following set segments:

$$p_7p_0: \quad b \;\; g\# \;\; e \;\; d\# \;\; a$$

$$i_{10}i_3: \quad d \;\; ab \;\; g \;\; eb \;\; c$$

The serially ordered pitch classes of the cyclic set are represented compositionally through the symmetries that ordering generates. Example 5.13a shows that symmetrically related dyads of sums 0 and 3 are literally represented in both pitch and rhythm in the unfolding

EXAMPLE 5.13

of the first two chords. The two sum-7 dyads, on the other hand, are symmetrically related only by pitch class (ex. 5.13b), and there is no symmetrical progression from the first sum-10 dyad, *d-ab*, to the second, *g-eb*, since *g* is omitted from the second chord. (I have never regarded such an omission—of only one of the two neighbor notes—as inconsistent with the principles of the system, but the omission of the axis note, or of both neighbor notes, would seem to be problematical, since this would mean that none of the symmetrical relationships that define the specific row form would be represented.) The opening figure of the second phrase (ex. 5.11B) unfolds the same two chords, in reverse order:

$$P_0P_7: \quad a \quad d\# \quad e \quad g\# \quad b$$

$$i_3i_{10}: \quad (c) \quad eb \quad g \quad ab \quad d$$

The third phrase retrospectively converts Example 5.11A into a "theme," by returning, after the rest that marks the midpoint of the

EXAMPLE 5.14

EXAMPLE 5.15

piece, to the opening "gesture," i.e., the contour and (approximate) rhythm assigned to the initial chord progression. However, this second statement of the theme (ex. 5.11C) unfolds a new chord progression (ex. 5.14):

$$p_7p_0: \quad c \ \boldsymbol{g} \ f \ / \ a\sharp \ \boldsymbol{a} \ d\sharp$$
$$i_{10}i_3: \quad e\flat \ \boldsymbol{g} \ a\flat \ / \ c\sharp \ \boldsymbol{a} \ f\sharp$$

The similarity between Examples 5.11A and 5.11C is an exclusively foreground phenomenon. In Example 5.15 I show an alternative version of 5.11C in which each chord of the new progression unfolds a symmetrical restatement of the parallel chord of the initial progression. The alternative version as a whole, however, does not symmetrically restate the theme, since there is no correspondence between the two progressions (exx. 5.12 and 5.14). Though at the time I composed this piece I could not have understood the beginning of the third phrase in the terms in which I describe it now, the performance direction, *hesitatingly*, implies an intuitive comprehension of its implications.

Example 5.11D refers to 5.11B in its return to the reversed sequence of the first two chords, and the resulting interchange of the two chords permits a literally inverted recapitulation of the theme (cf. ex. 5.12b).

From the very beginning I attributed a special significance to chords whose axis note shared the pitch class of a neighbor note, and which thus comprised only four rather than five pitch classes. I called these "tonic chords," and I saw them as pivots through which one could modulate to any one of three other arrays by assuming a different pitch-class duplication. The closing chord of the piece, for instance, is derived from axis note b:

$$p_7p_0: \quad g\# \quad \textbf{\textit{b}} \quad c\#$$
$$i_{10}i_3: \quad b \quad \textbf{\textit{b}} \quad e$$

Axis-note duplication of each of the remaining neighbor notes in turn converts the original array as follows:

$$p_9p_2: g\# \ \textbf{\textit{c\#}} \ c\# \quad p_7p_0: b \ \textbf{\textit{g\#}} \ e \quad p_3p_8: b \ \textbf{\textit{e}} \ e$$
$$i_0i_5: b \ \textbf{\textit{c\#}} \ e \quad i_4i_9: g\# \ \textbf{\textit{g\#}} \ c\# \quad i_0i_5: g\# \ \textbf{\textit{e}} \ c\#$$

For a deeper understanding of the implications of "tonic chords" I had to wait until 1969, when I found my first collaborator in developing this special approach to twelve-tone composition, exactly thirty years after my discovery of the cyclic set. This was a former pupil, Paul Lansky, now Professor of Music at Princeton University. Our work together during the next four years led to a radical expansion of the original theory and a vast enlargement of its compositional possibilities. Today I find myself unable to analyze my first "twelve-tone tonal" piece without reference to concepts of which I was not aware at the time of its composition and which only gradually evolved as a consequence of this collaboration.

For instance, the pitch-class collection that closes the second phrase

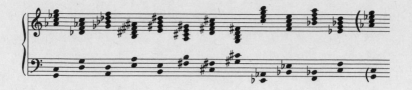

EXAMPLE 5.16

(ex. 5.11Z) is a repetition of one we have just heard in the second bar of the same phrase (ex. 5.11X). Surely it is just as much a "chord" as those that were derived in Example 5.6 as neighbor-note configurations of shared axis notes of the inversionally related forms of the cyclic set. But if we refer Examples 5.11X and 5.11Z to the alignment of the two row forms from which Example 5.6 is derived, we find the given pitch-class collection in the following conjunction of three-note segments:

$$p_7p_0: \quad b \ \textbf{\textit{g\#}} \ e$$
$$i_{10}i_3: \qquad g \ \textbf{\textit{eb}} \ c$$

Similarly, the intervening pitch-class collection (ex. 5.11Y) occurs as follows:

$$p_7p_0: \qquad d \ \textbf{\textit{f}} \ g$$
$$i_{10}i_3: \quad c \ \textbf{\textit{bb}} \ (f)$$

We can similarly reinterpret the first bar of the second phrase:

$$p_7p_0: \qquad e \ \textbf{\textit{d\#}} \ a$$
$$i_{10}i_3: \quad d \ \textbf{\textit{ab}} \ g$$

Why not regard these chords as deriving instead from new alignments of the inversionally related row forms? What we have been calling,

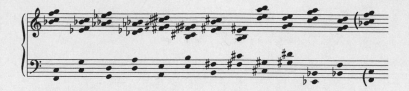

EXAMPLE 5.17

in the original alignment, an axis note will then be properly understood as a doubled note, an axis dyad of interval-o. By shifting $i_{10}i_3$
two degrees to the left relative to p_7p_0 we derive the chord of axis
interval-5, to which Examples 5.11X and 5.11Z belong (ex. 5.16), and
by shifting it two degrees to the right we derive the chords of axis
interval-7, to which Examples 5.11W and 5.11Y belong (ex. 5.17):

g c c g f d bb a d♯ e g♯ b c♯ f♯ f♯ c♯ b g♯ e d♯ a bb d f (g
eb g ab d c♯ a f♯ e b b e f♯ a c♯ d ab g eb c bb f f bb c (eb

g) c c g f d bb a d♯ e g♯ b c♯ f♯ f♯ c♯ b g♯ e d♯ a bb d f g
f) f bb c eb g ab d c♯ a f♯ e b b e f♯ a c♯ d ab g eb c bb f

In replacing the concept of the shared axis note by that of the shared
axis dyad we enlarge our concept of the array to include neighbor-
note configurations of every possible pairing of neighbor-note dyads.
In Example 5.18 the *g c c* segment of the p_7p_0 row is combined in turn
with each triadic segment of $i_{10}i_3$. The interval number of each axis
dyad is shown below the staff; the resulting neighbor-note configurations combine the *g-c* cyclic interval with each of its transpositions
(as indicated by the transposition numbers above the staff). A complete representation of the array on which my little piano piece is
based would comprise twelve series of symmetrically related pitch-

EXAMPLE 5.18

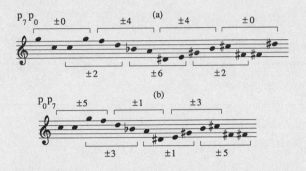

EXAMPLE 5.19

class collections, only three of which we have shown (respectively derived from axis intervals 0, 5, and 7) in Examples 5.6, 5.16, and 5.17. We should first of all correct our reading of Example 5.6, in view of our better understanding of the shared axis pitch-class as requiring representation by a pitch doubled at the unison or octave. And, in fact, this is how the doubled axis note seems largely to be represented in the composition, either through octave doubling, as in the first bar, or through symmetrical voice-leading, as in the connection between the first and second chords (ex. 5.13a) and in the convergence of the sum-10 dyad *ab-d* of the penultimate chord upon the *b* of the last chord.

Example 5.19 shows how overlapping tetrachordal segments of the interval-7 cyclic set will unfold every type of paired interval-7 dyads.

EXAMPLE 5.20

We now know that all of these tetrachordal collections[14] may be derived as neighbor-note chords. That derivation, unfolding the same
series of tetrachords, is represented in the two series of axis-dyad
chords shown in Example 5.20. Where in Examples 5.6, 5.16, and
5.17 an invariant difference is maintained between the cyclic intervals
for each series of neighbor-note collections and for each series of axis
intervals, in Example 5.20 an invariant pair of sums is maintained for
each series of neighbor-note collections and an invariant sum for each
series of axis dyads, which is to say that the series of neighbor-note
collections and the series of axis dyads each unfold symmetrically
rather than transpositionally. Though we have derived each chord in
the usual way, by combining a three-note segment of one form of the
set with a three-note segment of the other, the coincidental unfolding
of a tetrachordal segment of p_7p_0 (ex. 5.19) will mean that every
neighbor-note chord of Example 5.20a will comprise two dyads of
sum 7 and every neighbor-note chord of Example 5.20b two dyads

[14]We still call these "tetrachordal collections," even though some of them comprise
fewer than four pitch classes. Cf. pp. 111f., above.

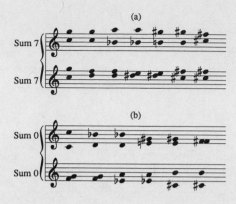

EXAMPLE 5.21

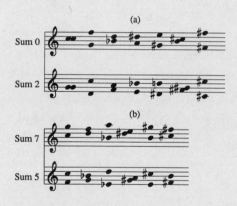

EXAMPLE 5.22

of sum 0 (ex. 5.21). The neighbor-note chords are additionally defined by a "secondary sum-couple," 0/2 for 5.20a and 7/5 for 5.20b
(ex. 5.22). The upper staff of Example 5.20a presents the complete
collection of tetrachords of sum-couples 7/7 and 0/2, the upper staff
of Example 5.20b the complete collection of tetrachords of sum-
couples 0/0 and 7/5. These are the invariant sum-couples. A tertiary
sum-couple, given by the paired cyclic intervals, is unique to each
specific neighbor-note collection.

Sum 3

Sum 10

EXAMPLE 5.23

Our earlier examples of axis-dyad chords were generated by align-
ing the two row forms so that the respective cycles were parallel to
each other. Thus Example 5.6 derived from a pairing of row forms
in which the vertically aligned neighbor notes showed a constant difference of 9 and the vertically aligned axis notes a constant difference
of 0, Example 5.16 from an alignment that showed alternate differences of 4 and 5, and Example 5.17 from an alignment that showed
alternate differences of 2 and 7. To find Example 5.20 in the paired
row forms these must be aligned so that the respective cycles move
in contrary motion to each other. Vertically aligned pitch classes will
now result in alternating constant sums of 7 and 3 for Example 5.20a:

g c c g f d b♭ a d♯ e g♯ b c♯ f♯ f♯ c♯ b g♯ e d♯ a b♭ d f (g
c e♭ g a♭ d c♯ a f♯ e b b e f♯ a c♯ d a♭ g e♭ c b♭ f f b♭ (c

and of 0 and 10 for Example 5.20b:

c c g f d b♭ a d♯ e g♯ b c♯ f♯ f♯ c♯ b g♯ e d♯ a b♭ d f g (c
c b♭ f f b♭ c e♭ g a♭ d c♯ a f♯ e b b e f♯ a c♯ d a♭ g e♭ (c

If the tetrachordal collections in Example 5.20 are special in that
they may be interpreted both as neighbor-note configurations of the
aligned row forms and as tetrachordal segments of the p_7p_0 (ex. 5.19),
so are the dyadic collections to which they are joined, since the latter
may be correspondingly interpreted both as the paired axis notes of
the aligned row forms and as dyadic segments of i_3i_{10} (ex. 5.23). Conversely, overlapping tetrachords of i_3i_{10} (ex. 5.24) may also be derived

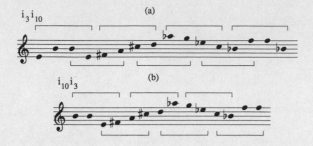

EXAMPLE 5.24

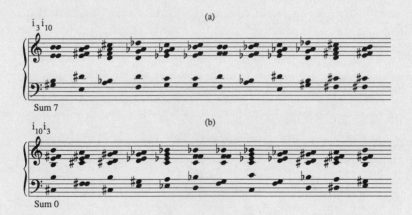

EXAMPLE 5.25

EXAMPLE 5.26

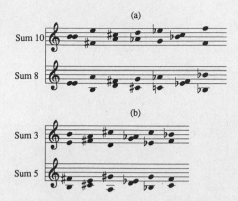

EXAMPLE 5.27

EXAMPLE 5.28

as neighbor-note chords (ex. 5.25) of primary sum-couple 3/3 or 10/
10 (ex. 5.26) and secondary sum-couple 10/8 or 3/5 (ex. 5.27). The
corresponding axis dyads will unfold the dyadic segments of p_7p_0 (ex.
5.28). Example 5.25a can be referred to the following alignment of
the two row forms:

b g# e d# a bb d f g c c g f d bb a d# e g# b c# f# f# c# (b
e b b e f# a c# d ab g eb c bb f f bb c eb g ab d c# a f# (e

and Example 5.25b to the following:

b c# f# f# c# b g# e d# a bb d f g c c g f d bb a d# e g# (b
b b e f# a c# d ab g eb c bb f f bb c eb g ab d c# a f# e (b

EXAMPLE 5.29

If we transpose each series of axis dyads and the corresponding series of neighbor-note configurations of Example 5.20 or 5.25 in opposite directions by the same interval, we derive another series of
combined three-note segments belonging to the same array. Suppose,
for example, that we transpose the axis dyads in Example 5.20a down
by a semitone and their respective neighbor-note collections up by a
semitone (ex. 5.29). The same two forms of the cyclic set, p_7p_0 and
i_3i_{10}, will now be represented in the following sum alignment:

g♯ b c♯ f♯ f♯ c♯ b g♯ e d♯ a b♭ d f g c c g f d b♭ a d♯ e (g♯
c♯ d a♭ g e♭ c b♭ f f b♭ c e♭ g a♭ d c♯ a f♯ e b b e f♯ a (c♯

These neighbor-note collections and their associated axis dyads no
longer unfold tetrachordal and dyadic segments of the respective row
forms from which they are derived. We can, however, deduce another
pair of inversionally related forms of the same cyclic set from this
series of axis-dyad chords (ex. 5.30). A second transposition of neighbor notes and axis dyads by complementary semitones will similarly
unfold a second pair of "resultant" inversionally related forms of the
cyclic set, and so on. Thus *all* transpositions of the two ("tonic") row
forms that generate the array are represented in the array:

$$p_7p_0 \quad p_9p_2 \quad p_{11}p_4 \quad p_1p_6 \quad p_3p_8 \quad p_5p_{10}$$
$$i_3i_{10} \quad i_1i_8 \quad i_{11}i_6 \quad i_9i_4 \quad i_7i_2 \quad i_5i_0$$

EXAMPLE 5.30

Each pair of resultant row forms may in turn be reinterpreted as tonic forms to generate a new array. The six arrays will be symmetrically related to each other—i.e., they are all in the same "key," which is to say that they all show the same sums (10 and 10) for the vertically aligned dyads of the paired row forms. They are in different modes, however, which is to say that they do not all show the same differences between aligned cyclic intervals:

$$P_0P_7 \quad P_2P_9 \quad P_4P_{11} \quad P_6P_1 \quad P_8P_3 \quad P_{10}P_5$$
$$\underline{i_3i_{10}} \quad \underline{i_1i_8} \quad \underline{i_{11}i_6} \quad \underline{i_9i_4} \quad \underline{i_7i_2} \quad \underline{i_5i_0}$$

$$9 \quad 9 \quad 1 \quad 1 \quad 5 \quad 5 \quad 9 \quad 9 \quad 1 \quad 1 \quad 5 \quad 5$$

All this is summed up in Example 5.31, which shows the neighbor-note collection of the same unison axis dyad for each array. As the example demonstrates, the first three of these arrays are transposed by a minor third in the last three. The special meaning of the minor-3rd transposition in twelve-tone tonality derives from the fact that the sum of four pitch-class numbers (or two dyadic sums) is not changed by the $+3$ or -3 transposition.

In each of these arrays, the cyclic intervals of the unison axis-dyad chords are separated by an odd interval number. Suppose we should

EXAMPLE 5.31

want them separated by an even interval number? This would necessitate the pairing of two row forms of the same aspect, rather than two inversionally related forms. (It was with this suggestion that Paul Lansky initiated our collaboration in the summer of 1969.) An "even" array can never be symmetrical to an "odd" array. Two arrays of the one type, however, which together show respectively complementary relations to an array of the other type, will establish a longer-range symmetrical relation:

$$p_0p_7: \quad c \quad c \quad \textbf{\textit{g}} \qquad p_0p_7: \quad c \quad c \quad \textbf{\textit{g}} \qquad i_{11}i_6: \quad \textbf{\textit{b}} \quad c \quad \textbf{\textit{f\#}}$$
$$i_{10}i_3: \quad b\flat \quad \textbf{\textit{c}} \quad e\flat \qquad p_{11}p_4: \quad b \quad \textbf{\textit{c}} \quad e \qquad i_{10}i_3: \quad b\flat \quad \textbf{\textit{c}} \quad e\flat$$

Through their shared sums, all the transpositions of the inversionally related row forms are comprehended in a closed system generated by a single repeated operation, analogous to the transpositions of the diatonic scale through the cycle of fifths:

p_0p_7:	c	c	g	f	d	$b\flat$	a	$d\#$	e	$g\#$	b	$c\#$	$f\#$	$f\#$
i_0i_5:	c	c	f	g	$b\flat$	d	$e\flat$	a	$g\#$	e	$c\#$	b	$f\#$	$f\#$
$p_{10}p_5$:	f	f	c	$b\flat$	g	$e\flat$	d	$g\#$	a	$c\#$	e	$f\#$	b	b
$i_{10}i_3$:	f	f	$b\flat$	c	$e\flat$	g	$a\flat$	d	$c\#$	a	$f\#$	e	b	b
p_8p_3:	$b\flat$	$b\flat$	f	$e\flat$	c	$a\flat$	g	$c\#$	d	$f\#$	a	b	e	e
i_8i_1:	$b\flat$	$b\flat$	$e\flat$	f	$a\flat$	c	$d\flat$	g	$f\#$	d	b	a	e	e
p_6p_1:	$e\flat$	$e\flat$	$b\flat$	$a\flat$	f	$d\flat$	c	$f\#$	g	b	d	e	a	a
i_6i_{11}:	$e\flat$	$e\flat$	$a\flat$	$b\flat$	$d\flat$	f	$f\#$	c	b	g	e	d	a	a
p_4p_{11}:	$a\flat$	$a\flat$	$e\flat$	$d\flat$	$b\flat$	$g\flat$	f	b	c	e	g	a	d	d
i_4i_9:	$a\flat$	$a\flat$	$d\flat$	$e\flat$	$g\flat$	$b\flat$	b	f	e	c	a	g	d	d
p_2p_9:	$c\#$	$c\#$	$g\#$	$f\#$	$d\#$	b	$a\#$	e	f	a	c	d	g	g
i_2i_7:	$c\#$	$c\#$	$f\#$	$g\#$	b	$d\#$	e	$b\flat$	a	f	d	c	g	g

As we can see from Example 5.20b, the "tonic" closing chord of my first "twelve-tone tonal" piece is only one of a family of twelve such chords, each characterized by an axis dyad of sum 10 (an axis dyad that therefore coincides with a segment of the tonic row form i_3i_{10}) and by a neighbor-note collection that duplicates the pitch-class content of a tetrachordal segment of the tonic row form p_0p_7. Chords that thus duplicate the segmental content of the paired row forms that generate all the chords of the array have special functions and hierarchical priority in the system.[15]

I have shown above how the collection of axis-dyad chords represented in Example 5.5 might be derived from either an interval-7 array:

$$p_0p_7: \quad a \quad d\# \quad e \ldots$$
$$i_1i_8: \quad b\flat \quad e\flat \quad f \ldots$$

[15]They have, for example, special significance as a means of modulating between different arrays, as is explained in *Twelve-Tone Tonality*.

EXAMPLE 5.32

or an interval-1 array:

$$p_0p_1: \quad a \quad d\# \quad b\flat \quad \ldots$$
$$i_7i_8: \quad e \quad e\flat \quad f \quad \ldots$$

The axis-dyad chords in Example 5.6, which are the harmonic basis of everything in my piano piece that is not comprised by the brackets w, x, y, and z, may be similarly derived, though not in the same sequence, from either the interval-7 array:

$$p_7p_0: \quad g \quad c \quad c \quad \ldots$$
$$i_{10}i_3: \quad b\flat \quad c \quad e\flat \quad \ldots$$

or an interval-3 array:

$$p_3p_0: \quad e\flat \quad c \quad c \quad \ldots$$
$$i_{10}i_7: \quad b\flat \quad c \quad g \quad \ldots$$

Where the interval-1 or interval-7 cyclic set generates an uninterrupted series of all twelve pitch classes, the interval-3 cyclic set falls into two partitions. A complete statement of the paired, inversionally related row forms, $p_3p_0/i_{10}i_7$, requires three partitions (ex. 5.32), as follows, in the axis interval-0 alignment:

$e\flat$ c c $e\flat$ a $f\#$ $f\#$ a $(e\flat \parallel e$ b $c\#$ d $b\flat$ f g $a\flat$ $(e \parallel f$ $b\flat$ d $c\#$ b e $a\flat$ g $(f$

$b\flat$ c g $e\flat$ e $f\#$ $c\#$ a $(b\flat \parallel b$ b $a\flat$ d f f d $a\flat$ $(b \parallel c$ $b\flat$ a $c\#$ $f\#$ e $e\flat$ g $(c$

This makes no difference to the compositional interpretation of the array in the first five and one-half bars of the piece. Any interval may generate a cyclic set, and arrays embracing all the cyclic intervals may be interrelated through intersections such as the above. The pairings of sets generated by *different* cyclic intervals, producing neighbor-note configurations comprising nonequivalent intervals, are also comprised in the system of twelve-tone tonality. There is, for example, a third interpretation of the collection of chords in Example 5.6, which would deduce them from an array of cyclic interval 2 and cyclic interval 4:[16]

$$b\flat \quad c \quad c \quad . \quad . \quad .$$
$$e\flat \quad c \quad g \quad . \quad . \quad .$$

Dissonant figuration is freely employed in my most recent compositions—a long delay in my coming to an understanding of this natural component of twelve-tone tonality that I now find it difficult to account for. Consider the passage from *Lulu* represented in Example 4.24:

> Symmetrical equivalence plays such a clearly referential role . . . as to suggest the possibility that such things as octave displacements, passing and neighbor notes, and suspensions can be defined in respect to it, just as these are defined in respect to the triad and scale-degree tendencies in the diatonic tonal system. Surely the figuration that we have added in Example [5.33] to the citation from *Lulu* in no way disrupts the harmonic sense of the passage.[17]

It is only since dissonant figuration has become an integral component of my compositional language that I have been able to offer what I think is a reasonable explanation for the interpolated *e* in the third chord of my piece, beginning with the *b♭* in the second bar (ex. 5.11):

$$p_0 p_7: \quad b\flat \quad d \quad f$$
$$i_3 i_{10}: \quad c\sharp \quad d \quad g\sharp$$

---

[16]Where the cyclic set derives from an even cyclic interval, both of its dyadic sums will be either even or odd. The two sums would be assigned opposite aspect names (cf. p. 135, above), $p_{10}i_0$ and i_3p_7 for the present array. If we choose to call the cyclic intervals 10 and 8, rather than 2 and 4, the two sets will be named p_0i_{10} and i_7p_3.

[17]Perle, "The First Four Notes of *Lulu*," in *The Berg Companion*, p. 28.

EXAMPLE 5.33

I believe the *e* to be a suspension, octave-displaced from the second chord, and would offer Example 5.34 as a background version of the first three chords.[18]

In my first article (1941) I proposed that twelve-tone composition had reached a stage in its development at which it was ready to move beyond the essentially primitive notion of an ostinato twelve-tone motive.[19] My principal work as a theorist and, above all, as a composer since then has concerned itself with discovering and developing

---

[18]A very different and much less convincing interpretation of this passage is given in *Twelve-Tone Tonality*, p. 31.

[19]The following comment on this first exposition of my theory is taken from *Perle on Perle*, p. 11: "My first article, in which I set forth my theory in the context of a critique of the twelve-tone system, was published at the same time [as my first piece in the system]. I wasn't ready to admit that the whole thing had originated in a misconception so I pretended that I had evolved my theory as a consequence of that critique, where in actuality the opposite was the case. I felt vaguely guilty about this piece of deceitfulness until a few years ago, when I read an essay by the British Nobel laureate Peter Medawar in which he shows that this is a regular and accepted procedure in the presentation of new scientific theories. That first paper of mine is embarrassingly naive in some ways, what with its attempts, fortunately brief and only in passing, to justify what I was doing in terms of 'overtones' and other nonsense, but I still consider its discussion of the problematical relation between the motivic and the extra-motivic functions of the series as valid and, considering when it was written, perceptive. This was, after all, still a time when there was hardly any interest in, let alone understanding of, the basic Schoenbergian concepts, and here I was already moving on in an entirely new direction from those same concepts. So perhaps there is nothing to be embarrassed about, especially when one considers the writings on the subject of twelve-tone music that were to be published in *Die Reihe* and elsewhere some twenty years later."

EXAMPLE 5.34

the implications of twelve-tone tonality, and not the least interesting result has been the realization of the extent to which these principles are anticipated in shared elements in the music of mainstream composers of the twentieth century—Scriabin, Stravinsky, Bartók, and Varèse, as well as Schoenberg, Berg, and Webern. The connections are evident not only in the extent to which the foundational concepts of the interval cycle and symmetrical inversion are shared, but also in all sorts of surprisingly detailed ways.

Consider the thematic tone-row of the first movement of the *Lyric Suite*. A dyadic segmentation is unequivocally asserted at its first appearance and repeatedly confirmed in the following bars:

$$P_5: f \ e \ | \ c \ a \ | \ g \ d \ | \ a\flat \ d\flat \ | \ e\flat \ g\flat \ | \ b\flat \ b$$

The same segmentation of the principal inverted row form would unfold another series of dyads:

$$I_{11}: b \ c \ | \ e \ g \ | \ a \ d \ | \ a\flat \ e\flat \ | \ d\flat \ b\flat \ | \ g\flat \ f$$

But in the recapitulation Berg substitutes the inversion for the prime in an alternative segmentation that is maximally invariant in dyadic pitch-class content with the prime, and that shows his awareness of the type of invariant relation through which, as we demonstrated above, the cyclic series establishes a closed system of row forms:

$$I_{11}: (b) \ | \ c \ e \ | \ g \ a \ | \ d \ a\flat \ | \ e\flat \ d\flat \ | \ b\flat \ g\flat \ | \ f \ b$$
$$P_5: (f) \ | \ e \ c \ | \ a \ g \ | \ d \ a\flat \ | \ d\flat \ e\flat \ | \ g\flat \ b\flat \ | \ b \ f$$

The first movement of Bartók's Fourth Quartet is, in a sense, in the same "key" as the first movement of the *Lyric Suite*. Let us lay out Berg's thematic row form as a succession of what I called "P/I dyads" in my second lecture, but keeping the dyads in their serial order:

$$f \quad c \quad g \quad a\flat \quad e\flat \quad b\flat$$
$$e \quad a \quad d \quad d\flat \quad g\flat \quad b$$

The "tonality" of the Bartók movement is based on these same six sum-9 dyads, which in this case are best represented as a scale, since their ordering in respect to each other is not precompositionally determined:

$$f \quad f\sharp \quad g \quad a\flat \quad a \quad b\flat$$
$$e \quad e\flat \quad d \quad d\flat \quad c \quad b$$

Since this ordering plays no structural role, as the ordering of Berg's dyads does, there is no basis for alternative interpretations such as there would have been had the same series of dyads unfolded as a cyclic set. For example, the following:

$$i_9 i_{10}: \quad e \; f \; f \; e \; f\sharp \; e\flat \; g \; d \; a\flat \; d\flat \; a \; c \; b\flat \; b \; b \; b\flat \; \ldots$$

might have been alternatively segmented into a series of sum-10 P/I dyads:

$$f \quad f\sharp \quad g \quad a\flat \quad a \quad b\flat \quad b$$
$$f \quad e \quad e\flat \quad d \quad d\flat \quad c \quad b$$

At the conclusion of the last movement of the Bartók Fifth Quartet the compositional context does, in fact, imply a cyclic interval. The following series of P/I (sum-7) dyads is unfolded in bars 763–777:

$$e \quad f \quad f\sharp \quad g \quad g\sharp$$
$$d\sharp \quad d \quad c\sharp \quad c \quad b$$

In bar 778 *g♯* moves to *a*, but the descent of the bass line is delayed, and it only descends to *b♭* together with the arrival of the top line at the same destination. A new series of P/I (sum–8) dyads is established at this point:

$$e \ f \ f\sharp \ g \ g\sharp \ a \ b\flat$$
$$e \ e\flat \ d \ c\sharp \ c \ b \ b\flat$$

The following interval-1 cyclic row form, embracing both, is implied:[20]

$$i_7 i_8\text{:} \ \ e\flat \ e \ e \ e\flat \ f \ d \ f\sharp \ c\sharp \ g \ c \ a\flat \ b \ a \ b\flat \ b\flat \ a \ \ldots$$

We have seen (p. 158, above) that two arrays that are not symmetrical with respect to each other can serve as components of a larger-range symmetrical structure in which the original asymmetrical relation is complemented. The first movement of Bartók's Fourth Quartet provides an example. A symmetrical basic cell of sum 3:

$$d \ e\flat$$
$$c\sharp \ c$$

regularly proceeds to a second symmetrical basic cell of sum 2:

$$d \ e$$
$$c \ b\flat$$

[20]There is a conjunction of both sums in the passage that concludes, at the change of tempo on the fourth bar from the end, with *d-f* in the cello and *f♯-d* in the remaining instruments. This is followed by a return to the sum-8 dyads alone and a final convergence on *b♭* (the initial pitch class of the work) in all the parts. Unfortunately, in later printings of the score the sum-7 component is eliminated a bar too early, by an unnamed editor's "correction" of the cello's *d-f* to *d-f♯*.

Symmetrical progressions play a significant role throughout the movement and in the structure of the movement as a whole, but this most important thematic and structural element, the conjunction of these two basic cells, is inherently asymmetrical, since one of the sums of complementation is odd and the other even. The two basic cells, regardless of their respective pitch levels, can never have the same axis of symmetry. Near the end of the movement, however, the progression is inverted, so the two asymmetrical progressions together form a larger symmetrical structure around sum 0:

$$c\ c\sharp\ d\ e\flat\ \|\ b\flat\ c\ d\ e$$
$$c\ b\ b\flat\ a\ \|\ d\ c\ b\flat\ a\flat$$

The concept of "resultant" row forms is anticipated in the twelve-tone music of both Webern and Berg. In the first movement of Webern's Quartet, Opus 22, for example, inversionally related row forms are simultaneously transposed by complementary intervals so as to maintain, through various permutations as to their order, the same P/I dyads of sum 0. The implied priority of inversional symmetry over set-structure as an integrative principle in twelve-tone music is carried even further in a large section of Act II, Scene 1 of *Lulu*, where the same sum of complementation is maintained for P/I dyads derived from different series, as well as from non-serial components.[21]

In my second lecture I showed how the minor-3rd transposition acquires a special relevance in certain works of Berg and Bartók through their exploitation of the pivotal functions of double-tritone tetrachords. The same transposition also has a special relevance to

[21]Douglas Jarman was the first to call attention to this, in "Dr. Schön's Five-Strophe Aria: Some Notes on Tonality and Pitch Association in Berg's *Lulu*," *Perspectives of New Music* VIII/2 (Spring–Summer 1970).

EXAMPLE 5.35   Perle, *Windows of Order*

twelve-tone tonality, as we have seen, though on a much larger scale and in a much more general sense.

The only example I have offered here of a composition that can be said to be *in* the system of twelve-tone tonality is my very first piece in the system, composed about fifty years ago. Though the "state of the art" has advanced far beyond this first attempt, and far beyond the tendencies in the same direction of the mainstream composers of the early years of this century, one can still sometimes discover, in the music of these composers, remarkably explicit anticipations of the current language of twelve-tone tonality.

Consider an excerpt (ex. 5.35) from a very recent work, my string quartet in one movement entitled *Windows of Order*. The passage is based on the alignments of a cyclic set of interval-6:

$$i_9p_3: \quad e \; f \; bb \; b \; (e \; || \; eb \; f\# \; a \; c \; (eb \; || \; d \; g \; g\# \; c\# \; (d$$

and a cyclic set of interval-2:

$$i_{11}p_1: \quad b \; c \; c\# \; bb \; eb \; ab \; f \; f\# \; g \; e \; a \; d \; (b$$

A complete "axis-dyad chord," derived by pairing a three-note segment of one set with a three-note segment of the other, occurs only at the beginning of the example:

$$i_9p_3: \quad d \quad g \quad g\sharp$$
$$i_{11}p_1: \quad g \quad e \quad a$$

The integers under each chord identify the "sum tetrachord" by its primary sum-couple. Thus the first chord in bar 218 combines a sum-9 dyad, *d-g*, from one set with a sum-11 dyad, *g-e*, from the other. The preceding *g♯-a* in the first violin extends this into a complete axis-dyad chord by interpreting *g-e* as an axis dyad and providing its remaining neighbor notes. The following tetrachords are not similarly extended into axis-dyad chords. The cyclic intervals are nevertheless implied in the shared sum-couples of these tetrachords.

Voice-leading possibilities in any progression of sum tetrachords derive from the differences between the combined sums of each of the four types of sum tetrachords comprised in an array. The present array gives us tetrachordal sums of 8 ($=9+11$), 10 ($=9+1$), 2 ($=3+11$), and 4 ($=3+1$). The difference between tetrachordal sums 8 and 10 in the first two chords of bar 218 is realized in the semitonal ascent of two parts against sustained notes in the other two, and the reversed progression from the fifth to the sixth chord is conversely realized. In the second half of the same bar the alternation of tetrachordal sums 4 and 2 is realized in the alternating whole steps in the cello against sustained notes in the other three parts. At the barline the same alternation of tetrachordal sums is reinterpreted, the difference of $+2$ becoming a difference of -10 in the descent of each of the three upper parts by -3 and the descent of the cello part by -1. The -3 descents are filled in by passing notes moving through segments of the interval-1 cycle.

Only the first and last chords in bar 220 are derived from the array.

EXAMPLE 5.36

The intervening chords are "dissonant" passing chords. Since the two principal chords share a primary sum-couple, their progression is symmetrical (ex. 5.36). The outer voices are octave-displaced in the second chord, however, and the space that is opened as a result is symmetrically partitioned in each part. There is nothing in this that is not already implied in the opening bars of Berg's Opus 3 (see pp. 112f., above).

The system of twelve-tone tonality is based entirely on two rigorously observed principles:

1. Pitch and pitch-class are referable only to the cyclic set—ultimately, the cyclic set of interval-1 or interval-7, since cyclic sets of any other interval number may be derived by cyclically partitioning either of these, a procedure that will be familiar to everyone who has studied the twelve-tone language of *Lulu*. Take, for example, the p_0p_7 form of the interval-7 cyclic set. Alternate pairs of pitch-class names will give us the two partitions of an interval-2 cyclic set:

C C g f D B♭ a d♯ E G♯ b c♯ F♯ F♯ c♯ b G♯ E d♯ a B♭ D f g (C

The specific row form thus derived unfolds dyadic sums 0 and 2:

C C D B♭ E G♯F♯ F♯ G♯ E B♭ D (C ‖ g f a d♯ b c♯ c♯ b d♯ a f g (g

Musical space may be symmetrically disposed in two ways: through interval cycles, and through inversional complementation. The cyclic set integrates both of these into a single concept. The symmetrical disposition of musical space is a natural consequence of the twelve-tone scale.

2. Harmonic relations conform to the only ordering principle provided by the system, the cyclic set. Symmetry is as referential to simultaneity in twelve-tone tonality as the triad is to simultaneity in diatonic tonality.

LECTURE VI *Tonal oder atonal?*

The "musical pilgrim's" journey in his "progress" from "Serialism" to "Minimalism" has not been a lonely one. He has had the company of a whole troop of fellow travelers, though they haven't all gotten off at the same station upon their "return to tonality." Nor was their point of departure the consequence of any great crisis in their personal relation to their art and its language, as it was for me in 1937 and, of course, for Schoenberg before that. As one reformed "Serialist" reports, he "grew up in a climate in which, for a composer, only dissonance and atonality were acceptable."[1] That climate was described in the Preface to the first edition (1962) of my *Serial Composition and Atonality*:

> The single most impressive musical development since World War II has been the astonishingly rapid and widespread dissemination of the practice of twelve-tone composition. In the very recent past the twelve-tone movement was regarded as the concern only of a few sectarians. Today it is no novelty to find the modern jazz artist improvising on a tone row, the young music student writing a twelve-tone piece for his composition class, the choreographer

[1]David Del Tredici, quoted in John Rockwell, *All American Music* (New York: Knopf, 1983), p. 77.

converting a twelve-tone classic into ballet music. It is only in the most backward circles that the mere use of a tone row will secure a composer's position as a member of the avant-garde, as it was sure to do only a few years ago.

In one of his late essays Schoenberg complained, "Advice for composing is delivered in the manner in which a cook would deliver recipes."[2] From the start he must have been apprehensive that his twelve-tone method would lend itself to just this sort of exploitation, and that is very likely why he did not make his method public until he was impelled to do so by Hauer's competitive promotion of his own twelve-tone method. It is also why I concluded the Preface to my book with the hope that it would make "the composition of twelve-tone music . . . more difficult." For Schoenberg, "the method of composing with twelve tones grew out of a necessity."[3] What was the necessity that brought so many young, and some not so young, composers to it thirty and forty years later, and the further necessity that led to their subsequent "return to tonality"? Why should Luciano Berio have had to wait until 1959 to discover that "serial procedure guarantees nothing"?[4] Schoenberg had said the same thing thirty-five years earlier.

A sympathetic historian of modern music offers the following description of one contemporary composer's pilgrimage: "[He] went through a common history of post-Schoenbergian and post-Webernian serialism in the fifties and early sixties. . . . He came to realize, as he has written, 'that the music of the "old masters" was a

[2]Arnold Schoenberg, "The Blessing of the Dressing," in *Style and Idea* (1975), p. 386.

[3]Arnold Schoenberg, "Composition with Twelve Tones," in *Style and Idea* (1975), p. 216.

[4]Quoted in Glenn Watkins, *Soundings: Music in the Twentieth Century* (New York: Schirmer Books, 1988), p. 522.

living presence, that its spiritual values had not been displaced or de-
stroyed by the new music.' And so he was led . . . to write what
amount to recompositions of the past, of Mahler and late Beethoven
in particular."[5] In 1925, responding to the very different rapproche-
ment with the past represented by the neo-classic movement, Schoenberg composed his *Three Satires*, Opus 28, a setting for mixed chorus
of his own polemical texts. The first of these, "At the Crossroads,"
ironically poses the question, "Tonal oder atonal?" In his Preface
Schoenberg takes special aim "at those who vainly strive for a 'return
to . . .' . Such a person should not pretend that it is up to him to decide
how far back he will soon be finding himself, or that he establishes
an alliance between himself and one of the great masters by this
means." Whatever the current relevance of these words, the notion
that the constant reiteration of a conventional harmonic progression
represents a "return to tonality," or that a collage of quotations from
the music of the "old masters" will restore their "living presence,"
can hardly be equated with the ways in which the neo-classic composers who were the targets of Schoenberg's *Satires* interpreted and
implemented their "back to Bach" slogan, or the ways in which Stravinsky allied himself with Pergolesi or Tchaikovsky.

　　Minimalism and collage "composition" are grotesque parodies of
tonality that testify to its demise, not to its revival. What has happened to "tonality" that it should be in need of revival? The reviv-
alists' work ought to begin with the answer to this question, which
it doesn't even occur to them to ask. A contest for compositions "in
any style which relies partially or wholly on any major/minor key
systems or modes" is not likely to contribute very much to the revival
of "tonality." Does one *choose* whether or not to be a "tonal" composer? The very notion that this is a matter of choice is self-

---

[5]Paul Griffiths, *Modern Music*, pp. 200f., on George Rochberg.

EXAMPLE 6.1   Mahler, Symphony No. 9, 1st mvt.

destructive—an admission that the tonal system of the past is no longer an authentic, viable, self-contained musical language. One may borrow it, and borrow from it, but one makes an authentic statement in doing so only insofar as that statement does not pretend to constitute a revival. The tonal revivalist is immediately faced with a decision that is impossible to make and that it is dishonest to avoid. How much of the tonal tradition is he going to revive? Is the restored tradition to include the progression from the second movement of Mahler's Ninth Symphony that I quoted in Example 3.5 but not the variant that follows it? It would undoubtedly include the expository statement of the principal theme of the first movement of Mahler's Ninth (ex. 6.1a), but what about its recapitulation (ex. 6.1b)? In view of what happened to the tonal tradition, wouldn't it be wise to excise such threats to its integrity as the beginning of the *Faust Symphony* (ex. 2.5), or the Bergian cyclic progression from Chopin's Eb Major Prelude (ex. 3.33)?

If I am not sympathetic to the rehabilitated tonality of reformed twelve-tone composers, this is not meant to imply that I have revised my original critique of the twelve-tone system. I still find, as I did in 1939, an inherent contradiction in the concept of a twelve-tone series which, in Schoenberg's words, "functions in the manner of a motive" and must thus "be invented anew for each piece," but which must at the same time "substitute for some of the unifying and formative advantages of scale and tonality."[6] Surely, whatever there is about the twelve-tone series that can "substitute for some of the unifying and formative advantages of scale and tonality" need not—indeed, *must not*—"be invented anew for each piece." The problem of distinguishing between the "motive" and its frame of reference in twelve-tone music has always been tacitly acknowledged in the work of those composers who found ways of coping with this problem, just as they had found ways of coping with the special problems of preserial atonal composition, but in thus coping they have only perpetuated the situation Schoenberg hoped to transcend with his formulation of the serial concept in the first place, for it was just these special problems that had led him, as he said, to lay "the foundations for a new procedure in musical construction which seemed fitted to replace those structural differentiations provided formerly by tonal harmonies."[7]

Scriabin's definitive break with the diatonic tonal system occurred at the same time as Schoenberg's, but, unlike the Viennese school, Scriabin bypassed "free" atonal composition entirely and proceeded at once to a "new procedure in musical construction" that was intended to "substitute for some of the unifying and formative advantages of scale and tonality." Though Scriabin was not the first to employ the octatonic scale, he was the first to employ it as a *set*,[8] a strictly defined and exclusive collection of pitch-class relations that served simultaneously as chord and scale, as the sole criterion of simultaneity,

[6]Schoenberg, "Composition with Twelve Tones," pp. 218, 219.
[7]Ibid., p. 218.
[8]Though Scriabin was the first to use the octatonic scale as a set, he was not the first to use a set. In Debussy's piano prelude *Voiles*, the black-key pentatonic pitch-class collection as employed in the middle section and the $C2_0$ pitch-class collection as employed in the outer sections conform to the following description of a pitch-class set.

EXAMPLE 6.2

and the sole explicit criterion of linear succession as well—for linearity, in Scriabin's system, is rarely more than the unfolding of successive octatonic components as "broken chords." Most of us, I think, have occasionally encountered a musically uneducated improvisor at the piano who has discovered that whatever he does will sound "right" so long as he sticks to the black keys. He is improvising on a pitch-class set, the pentatonic scale. A similar restriction to the notes of a diminished-7th chord will offer similarly guaranteed, though even less interesting, results. But an expansion of the set to *two* diminished-7th chords vastly enlarges the musical possibilities without in any way limiting the guarantee of "rightness." Two diminished-7th chords together will give us one of the symmetrical partitionings of the octatonic collection. Like the diminished-7th chord itself, the octatonic scale is statable at three non-equivalent transpositional levels. Each of these intersects with the other two through one or another of its diminished-7th chord components (ex. 6.2). The two remaining tritone-divisible tetrachords (cf. pp. 47f., above) give us alternative symmetrical partitionings of the same scale (ex. 6.3). In the Seventh Sonata Scriabin derives from the octatonic scale a symmetrical tetrachord that contains no tritone and that may

EXAMPLE 6.3

EXAMPLE 6.4

therefore be paired with its tritone transposition to complete the octatonic aggregate (ex. 6.4).

Scriabin's systematic employment of the octatonic scale as the basis
of a consistent and self-contained post-diatonic musical language is in
no way analogous to its use by Bartók as an alternative "atonal"
means of pairing Dorian tetrachords in No. 33 of the *44 Violin Duets*,
or to its occasional and incidental use by Berg within the larger
twelve-tone context of *Lulu*. As to Stravinsky's astonishingly extensive exploitation of octatonic elements,[9] it is to be distinguished from
Scriabin's octatonicism in the same way as Stravinsky's unfolding of
the C3 cycle in the Introduction to *Le Sacre* is to be distinguished from
Varèse's in *Density 21.5* (pp. 82f., above).

The great virtue, for Scriabin, of the octatonic scale was precisely
the fact that it did *not* need to "be invented anew for each piece." Together, the three transpositions of the octatonic scale comprise a two-
fold representation of the twelve-tone aggregate. The octatonic sys-

[9]Van den Toorn, *The Music of Igor Stravinsky*.

EXAMPLE 6.5

tem was Scriabin's personal solution to the problem of twelve-tone composition. Half a dozen years or so after Scriabin's death, Schoenberg came up with the principle of ordering and Hauer with the principle of partitioning as means of differentiating representations of the universal set of twelve pitch classes from one another, the foundational requirement for a twelve-tone system. Scriabin's sketches for his projected "Prefatory Action" show that in the last year of his short life he was already preoccupied with the same problem. Among these sketches we find a set of the twelve pitch classes derived by the addition of a diminished-7th chord to the octatonic partitioning shown in Example 6.3a, a formation (ex. 6.5a) that corresponds to one of the basic twelve-tone tropes of *Lulu* (ex. 6.5b), in which the diminished-7th chord is added to the octatonic partitioning shown in Example 6.3b.[10]

In one of his posthumously published lectures on "the new music" Webern described his intuitive anticipation of the notion of ordering as a means of defining the twelve-tone aggregate:

What happened? I can only relate something from my own experience; about 1911 I wrote the "Bagatelles for String Quartet" (Op. 9), all very short pieces, lasting a couple of minutes—perhaps the shortest music so far. Here I had the feeling, "When all twelve

[10]Perle, "Scriabin's Self-Analyses," pp. 119ff.

notes have gone by, the piece is over." Much later I discovered that
all this was a part of the necessary development. In my sketchbook
I wrote out the chromatic scale and crossed off the individual notes.
Why? Because I had convinced myself, "This note has been there
already." . . . In short, a rule of law emerged; until all twelve notes
have occurred, none of them may occur again. The most important
thing is that each "run" of twelve notes marked a division within
the piece, idea or theme.[11]

A strict observance of such a "rule of law" would limit a composition, if it were not to terminate "when all twelve notes have gone by,"
to the constant reiteration of a single permutation of the twelve pitch
classes. In fact, Webern's first twelve-tone work, *Drei Volkstexte*,
Opus 17 (1924), hardly progresses beyond this "crossing off"
method. Each of the three movements is based on a single reiterated
form of a different tone row. The same "rule of law" is invoked by
Schoenberg as an explanation of another rule, that "only one set
should be used in one composition": "The use of more than one set
was excluded because in every following set one or more tones would
have been repeated too soon."[12] But such a formulation of the principle of non-repetition contradicts the basic postulates of Schoenberg's own twelve-tone system, since it would equally exclude transposition of the set or its employment in more than one of its four
aspects. Clearly, the ordering of the twelve pitch classes that results
from the "rule of law" that "until all twelve notes have occurred,
none of them may occur again" is a means of defining the twelve-
tone aggregate, and it is only to this aggregate that the rule of non-
repetition applies.

But ordering is not the only means of assigning a pitch-class struc-

[11]Webern, *The Path to the New Music*, p. 51.
[12]Schoenberg, "Composition with Twelve Tones," p. 219.

ture to the twelve-tone aggregate, and it has never been a sufficient means. The division of the aggregate into unordered segments— what Hauer called "tropes"[13]—is another means, and its division into symmetrically related dyads (which, however, requires pitch-class duplication at the points of intersection for any even axis of symmetry) is a third. The notion of ordering derives from the concept of the twelve-tone set as a unitary, i.e., an unsegmented structure, but it is only in the most primitive of twelve-tone serial compositions that the set has been so conceived. Surely it is the harmonic content of the six four-note chords that open Schoenberg's Piano Piece, Opus 33a, and the symmetrical relation between the first three and the last three of these chords that make sense to us as listeners and that we subsequently recall. That sense is not compromised by the impossibility of determining which of the 13,824 different twelve-tone rows that can be segmented into these chords is their actual source. And where we hear and recall a twelve-tone set as a linearly ordered structure, we are either faced with a contradiction between the motivic and the extra-motivic functions of the row, or ordering itself turns out to be subordinate to another property of the set, such as voice-leading relations, as in the third movement of the *Lyric Suite* (see pp. 93f., above), or symmetry, as in the first movement of the *Lyric Suite* and in the Webern Symphony. In each of the latter the ordering of the complete series is determined by the ordering of its first six elements, since the second half of the set is the T(6) retrograde of the first half. It is further determined by inversionally symmetrical relations within the set. The sum-9 dyadic segmentation in the first movement of the *Lyric Suite* was shown in Example 4.25. Webern's series may be reinterpreted so that its hexachordal P/R symmetry (ex. 6.6a) is displaced

[13]J. M. Hauer, *Vom Melos zur Pauke* (Vienna: Universal Edition, 1925); *Zwölftontechnik* (Vienna: Universal Edition, 1926).

EXAMPLE 6.6

by tetrachordal P/I symmetry (ex. 6.6b), with each tetrachord sym-metrical around the same axis of sum 3 for the principal prime form of the row.

The preoccupation with ordering in the post-Schoenbergian evo-lution of serial composition has been, to my mind, a preoccupation with what is ultimately a secondary and superficial aspect of Schoen-berg's twelve-tone "method."[14] Arbitrary and artificial constraints imposed by the ordering principle have been countered by the im-position of other arbitrary and artificial extensions of the same prin-ciple. By applying various arithmetical procedures to the order and pitch-class numbers of the notes, an endless "variety" of set trans-formations beyond those conceived by Schoenberg may be derived. The notion of ordering has been extended to rhythm and dynamics, and even to other "parameters," as a way of arriving at a "total" or "integral" serialism. This necessitated the invention of bizarre and

[14]It is not, however, a superficial aspect of twelve-tone tonality. The alternative ad-jacency sums of the cyclic series derive from the strict ordering of the series, but that ordering is a *background* structure, implied in its entirety by any three-note segment of the series.

arbitrary precompositional constructs such as durational scales of twelve note-values and intensity scales of twelve dynamic levels. As John Backus concludes in his remarks on Boulez's *Structures*: "What results can only be described as composition by numerology. The possibilities are endless; a computer could be programmed to put down notes according to this prescription and in a very short time could turn out enough music to require years for its performance. By using different numerical rules—using a knight's move, for example, rather than the bishop's move along the diagonals—music for centuries to come could be produced."[15] As the inventor of the "Digionic Synthesizer" puts it: "With serial music we can take thirteen tones, plug them into this, and you get 4000 permutations immediately. Why should a composer waste his time making permutations?" And is it really not self-evident that there is no analogy between our perception of pitch intervals and dynamic intervals? What is the octave of a *mezzo forte*? Is it not self-evident that between our tolerance of deviations from the ratio of 2 : 1 in pitch octaves and in Stockhausen's "duration octaves" there is no relation whatever? What is the pitch-succession equivalent of an *accelerando*? Such extensions of Schoenberg's twelve-tone system have more relevance to the invention of cryptographic codes than to musical composition.

It is hardly surprising that "composition by numerology" should have found its analog, in much of what passes for contemporary music theory today, in analysis by numerology. "Pitch classes are equated with pitch-class *numbers*, intervals with interval *numbers*, and ostensible observations about musical relations turn out to be trivial observations about the collection of integers, modulo 12."[16] Questions of spacing, doubling, and voice-leading are entirely eliminated,

[15]John Backus, "Die Reihe—A Scientific Evaluation," *Perspectives of New Music* I/1 (Fall 1962): 170.

[16]Perle, review of Maegaard, *Studien*, p. 282.

EXAMPLE 6.7

and what are put forth as statements about notes are in effect statements about subsets of unassigned numbers. And, most appalling of all, the current "return to tonality" seems to be finding its counterpart, not in the abandonment of this kind of analysis, but in its extension to tonal music.

Boulez and Stockhausen were only the most prominent of the serialist composers who finally decided that they had reached a dead end and went on to other things, such as chance composition. The "return to tonality" is mainly the work of more recently reformed serialists. We still have a good number of unreformed serialists with us, however, who persist in their preoccupation with pitch-class ordering, a preoccupation which is only a consequence of a more fundamental misconception. Ordering has no function other than that of unfolding the twelve-tone aggregate, but the aggregate it unfolds is only a surface manifestation, as primitive relative to a really integral and autonomous twelve-tone language as the constant surface reiteration of the diatonic scale would be relative to the traditional tonal system.

Would the first movement of the *Lyric Suite* have been a more authentically twelve-tone composition if Berg had supplied, in the sequential passage quoted in Example 4.5, the eight "missing" notes of each of the twelve-tone row forms that are represented in this passage only by their initial four-note segments? The principal set-form of the twelve-tone trope that represents the Countess Geschwitz in Berg's *Lulu* is shown in Example 6.7. Though segment C is an integral component of the set, it also occurs throughout the opera independently

EXAMPLE 6.8

of Countess Geschwitz's Trope, as one of the three Basic Cells of the work. Its principal form and pitch level are the same, in that capacity, as they are where the same pentachord occurs as a segment of Example 6.7. Three statements of this trope are represented in the concluding bars of the opera. Two of these are inversionally related (ex. 6.8) and share the same perfect-5th segment, *a-e*. The Basic Cell in its "home key," of which *a-e* is a component, simultaneously unfolds in the bass line (ex. 6.9). As a segment of Countess Geschwitz's Trope, this form of the Basic Cell requires, for the completion of the twelve-tone aggregate, the remaining segments of the principal form of the Trope as shown in Example 6.7. But only Segment B is presented. The replacement of the perfect-5th segment, *g-d*, of the principal form of Countess Geschwitz's Trope by its major-2nd transposition in the final bars, so that it is absorbed into Segment C, creates the effect of a long-range cadential resolution at the conclusion of the op-

EXAMPLE 6.9

era, a resolution which coincides with the completion of the long-range voice-leading progression described on page 99, above, and illustrated in Example 4.11. Would *Lulu* have been a more authentically twelve-tone composition if Berg had supplied the two "missing" notes, *g-d*, of the twelve-tone aggregate in this final statement of Countess Geschwitz's Trope?

Not only does Berg neglect to complete the aggregate by supplying the "missing" segment of Countess Geschwitz's Trope, but he also enlarges the extent to which that set is deficient in its last appearance in the opera, by interpolating notes that are extraneous to it. In the third bar of Example 6.9 the descending statement of Segment B is interrupted after only four of its five notes, *ab-gb-eb-db*, have sounded. The unfolding of Segment B is resumed with the repetition of *eb-db* at the octave below, then interrupted again by another octave transposition and a second repetition of *eb-db*, and finally completed by the

twice postponed *b♭*. The gap between the initial *e♭-d♭* and its first octave transposition is filled in by the remaining notes of the whole-
tone cycle of which this dyad is a component.

As Schoenberg said, his "method of composing with twelve tones
grew out of a necessity." I see that "method"—the constant reiteration of an ordered twelve-tone aggregate—as the desperate act of a
man who has lost his way in a forest and who wisely concludes, unlike the protagonist of *Erwartung*, that his best plan will be to walk
straight ahead in a single direction, rather than to move about at ran-
dom in the hope of eventually finding a shorter way out of the
woods.

Bartók followed another path on his way toward an integral
twelve-tone language:

> The outcome of these studies [of folk music] was of decisive influ-
> ence upon my work, because it freed me from the tyrannical rule
> of the major and minor keys. . . . It became clear to me that the
> old modes, which had been forgotten in our music, had lost noth-
> ing of their vigour. . . . This new way of using the diatonic scale
> brought freedom from the rigid use of the major and minor keys,
> and eventually led to *a new conception of the chromatic scale, every tone*
> *of which came to be considered of equal value and could be used freely and*
> *independently* [emphasis added].[17]

I quoted Bartók earlier on the "invariably tonal" basis of "our peasant
music" (pp. 46f.). This tonal basis was of equally "decisive influence"
and did not stand in opposition to the "free" and "independent" use
of all twelve tones. For Bartók the involvement of his compositional
language with folk music was perhaps a way of maintaining the "reality of thought" and the "sense of action" of which Hannah Arendt

[17]Béla Bartók, "Autobiography," *Tempo*, no. 13 (1949) [trans. of "Selbstbiogra-
phie," 1921]; reprinted in Bartók, *Béla Bartók Essays*, p. 410.

speaks in her essay on "Tradition and the Modern Age": "Our tradition of political thought began when Plato discovered that it is somehow inherent in the philosophical experience to turn away from the common world of human affairs; it ended when nothing was left of this experience but the opposition of thinking and acting, which, depriving thought of reality and action of sense, makes both meaningless."[18]

The reading of the tone row of the third movement of the *Lyric Suite* as a series of pitch classes (ex. 4.1) rather than of pitches (ex. 4.3) deprives it of its voice-leading implications and thus deprives musical thought of reality and musical action of sense. It may not be necessary any longer to insist that an analysis of a twelve-tone composition in terms of serial ordering alone is insufficient, but it is surely time to recognize that an invocation merely of principles of invariance is only a partial corrective. Voice-leading procedures are repeatedly stressed in both volumes of my book on the Berg operas, but particularly in the volume on *Lulu* (see exx. 4.10 and 4.11, above). The special nature of voice-leading relations in *Lulu* and the special harmonic character of the work are interdependent.

In *Lulu*, harmonic formations derived from *various* twelve-tone sets are components of a pervasive harmonic texture to which the sets themselves are subordinate and which comprises non-dodecaphonic elements as well. How far this texture departs from that of other twelve-tone music is suggested in the character of the outer voices, and especially of the bass line, whose linearity and directed motion imply a significant affiliation to traditional tonal music in spite of the radical difference in harmonic content.[19]

[18]Hannah Arendt, *Between Past and Future* (1961; reprint ed., New York: Penguin, 1977), p. 25.
[19]Perle, *The Operas of Alban Berg*. Vol. 2: *Lulu*, p. 86.

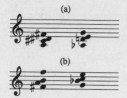

EXAMPLE 6.10

EXAMPLE 6.11   Schoenberg, Op. 33a

Copyright 1929 by Universal Edition. Copyright renewed 1956 by Gertrude Schoenberg. Used by permission of Belmont Music Publishers.

But this "other twelve-tone music" is by no means devoid of voice-leading implications, and it may even be that we are at least as dependent on these as we are on our recognition of invariant relations among different set forms for whatever it is in this music that we really "comprehend," in the ordinary sense in which this term has relevance to the listening experience. The two chords in Example 6.10a are not simply contiguous to each other; they are a progression in which the first chord moves to the second through a semitonal inflection of each of its elements. The same progression is reversed and inverted in Example 6.10b. These voice-leading implications are not eliminated by the twelve-tone compositional context in the opening bars of Schoenberg's Opus 33a, in spite of the octave displacement of the second chord of Example 6.10b (ex. 6.11). In Example 6.12a we see a compositional interpretation of two P/I dyads of sum 3. A sec-

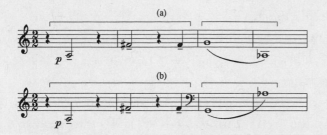

EXAMPLE 6.12

ond interpretation (ex. 6.12b) gives us the opening figure of the Webern Symphony. The displacement by two octaves of one of the two
notes of the second dyad doesn't eliminate the voice-leading relations
that derive from the shared axis of symmetry of the two dyads. In
fact, it is only thanks to voice-leading and symmetry that we are able
to preserve for twelve-tone music such an essential and familiar aspect
of traditional compositional practice as octave displacement—which
is not to imply an equation between intervallic qualities in twelve-
tone music and in tonally functional triadic music.[20]

There remains a crucial distinction between the role of voice-
leading in Berg's twelve-tone practice and in that of Schoenberg and
Webern. The filling-in of the octave that separates the repeated *eb-db*
in the third bar of Example 6.9 is a voice-leading procedure. In its
interpolation of a cyclic pitch structure that is extraneous to the given
twelve-tone set we again see, as we did in Example 4.5, how in Berg's
music voice-leading may take precedence over what Schoenberg and
Webern would have regarded as inviolable axioms of twelve-tone
composition.

Symmetry is as central to what I call twelve-tone tonality as the
triad and the key center are to the major/minor system, and the mean-

[20]Cf. Perle, *Serial Composition and Atonality*, pp. 30f.

ing I impute to the term "tonality" in "twelve-tone tonality" derives only from the presence of an analogously central and all-pervasive principle and not from any other shared properties of the two systems, though there certainly are such shared properties. But to move from the abstract precompositional structure of triadic and tonal relations to the composition itself means to interrupt and then to restore those relations. The same thing is true of symmetry in twelve-tone tonality. It is only in the precompositional array that this symmetry is always literally and uninterruptedly unfolded. The compositional interpretation of the precompositional symmetrical array constantly interrupts and restores that symmetry.

In the last of a series of wise and brilliant lectures that Roger Sessions presented at the Juilliard School in 1949 he spoke of "the way that apparently self-sufficient currents of development coincide in a single historical movement. Different sets of facts, having no apparent connection with each other, seem over and over again to coincide in such a manner that it is tempting to seek, or perhaps to assume, connections and to find only specious reasons for them. Fundamental and far-reaching changes in one so-called 'field' of human activity are likely to coincide with changes of an equally far-reaching character in many others." In spite of these evident connections, the "process of musical development [is one] which we can interpret in terms of music alone" and which we can explain as "the inevitable consequence of developments which had been taking place within the most self-contained musical sphere."[21]

It is without being tempted to seek any reasons for it that I call attention to the fact that the concept of symmetry seems to have the same far-reaching significance in many other " 'fields' of human activity" in our time that it has in music. Indeed, according to some

[21]Sessions, *Musical Experience*, pp. 105f.

cosmologists, symmetry and "broken" symmetry—what I have called "interrupted" symmetry in differentiating between actual musical compositions and the perfect background symmetry of interval cycles and inversional relations—may even take us all the way back to the "big bang." Here is Timothy Ferris on the creation of the universe:

> The mathematical symmetries that the unified theories have exposed at the foundations of natural law are more subtle and complex than those of snowflakes, but their principle is the same. They imply that we live in a crystallized universe of broken symmetries. Perfect symmetry may be beautiful, but it's also sterile. Perfectly symmetrical space means nothingness. As soon as you introduce an object into that space, you break the symmetry. . . . Perfectly symmetrical time means that nothing can happen. As soon as you have an event, then you break the symmetry. . . . It may even be that we owe the very origin of our universe to the imperfection of the breaking of the absolute symmetry of absolute emptiness.[22]

I have stressed, throughout these lectures, the connections between us and those whom I have called the mainstream composers of the twentieth century, in whose work the revolutionary implications of the change from the diatonic scale to the symmetrical twelve-tone scale was first manifested, and the connections between them and the tonal heritage that formed them and from which they broke away. It is they, and only they, who are the authentic "avant-garde" of our time. Our task is still what Roger Sessions said it was forty years ago, to appraise and consolidate the revolution they made.

If folk music was of "decisive influence" for Bartók because it "freed [him] from the tyrannical rule of the major and minor keys,"

[22]Timothy Ferris, *The Creation of the Universe: A Science Special for Television* (Pasadena: Northstar Associates, 1985).

other composers—Scriabin and the Vienna circle—found that same freedom in other ways. The path to an understanding of even the most esoteric of these composers is not through what sets them apart but through what connects them with their contemporaries and with the great tradition that was their common heritage.

But it is precisely these connections that we are told we must abjure if we are ever to make anything of atonal and twelve-tone music. According to John Rahn's useful textbook, *Basic Atonal Theory*, the " 'tonal filters' " which enable us to comprehend the music of Bach, Beethoven, and Brahms "are worse than useless" for an understanding of the new music. "The theory of atonal music should build you a set of 'atonal filters,' " through which you can come to comprehend "the relational structures of pitch, duration, etc., involved in 'non-tonal' Western music."[23] Accessibility to this music, presumably, is to be reserved for a special class of listeners who have the professional education and experience to read theoretical treatises on atonal music. The extended definition of "tonality" proposed by the Schenkerian theorist Felix Salzer comprises

> within its orbit . . . works as contrasting as a motet of the thir-teenth century and compositions by Machaut, Dufay, Frescobaldi, Mozart, Wagner, Debussy or Bartók. This language far transcends the style of specific periods and of certain composers because it is able to find expression in the most divergent styles and settings. In whatever style this musical language happens to express itself, whether in instrumental music, in song or opera, whether the style is gothic, baroque, classic or impressionistic, the basic character-istics of musical direction, continuity and coherence are the same and constitute a common denominator. . . . Structural or tonal music allows for the greatest possible variety, elasticity and indi-

[23]John Rahn, *Basic Atonal Theory* (New York: Schirmer Books, 1980), pp. 1ff.

viduality within the fundamental principles of structural direction and organization as represented in any period from the twelfth to the twentieth century.

The only music that Salzer can cite as representative of different "possibilities of musical coherence and continuity" is that of "Schönberg and his development of the twelve-tone system."[24] The music psychologist and aesthetician Victor Zuckerkandl finds that principles of musical perception that are otherwise universally relevant don't apply to twelve-tone music. "With the new music, the key changes with every step; each interval has, so to speak, its own center of reference. The interval becomes absolute, stands wholly on its own, and expresses nothing but the relation between two tones of different pitch."[25] I have yet to discover the "atonal filters" that would make such a music comprehensible to me.

Throughout these talks I have discussed the music of Scriabin, Bartók, Varèse, and Stravinsky in the same purview as the atonal and twelve-tone music of Schoenberg, Berg, and Webern, though not without making distinctions. I would go even further. The whole-tone scale, like the twelve-tone scale, divides the octave symmetrically, and wherever the whole-tone scale generates a self-contained complex of pitch relations it is only as an adjunct of total chromaticism that it does so. The whole-tone system is a subdivision of what I should have liked to call the "twelve-tone system" if that term had not already been taken over to refer to the more limited notion of music based on the Schoenbergian twelve-tone row. The extensive whole-tone sections of Debussy's *Voiles* and of the second movement of Rimski-Korsakov's *Le Coq d'or Suite* are a kind of twelve-tone

[24]Felix Salzer, *Structural Hearing* (1952; reprint ed., New York: Dover, 1962), pp. 282f.
[25]Zuckerkandl, *Man the Musician*, p. 118.

music, since the symmetrical scale on which these are based can only be understood as a partition of the twelve-tone scale.

The pervasive employment of all the diatonic modes in the music of Bartók and early Stravinsky is assimilated to symmetrical harmonic relations whose only source is likewise to be found in the symmetrical structure of the twelve-tone scale. Folk songs, though their own character is inherently diatonic and tonal, can be strikingly integrated into a larger symmetrical context, as we have seen in the Introduction to *Le Sacre du printemps* and the Bartók Duet No. 33. In his book on Bartók Elliott Antokoletz devotes a whole chapter to the composer's "Symmetrical Transformations of the Folk Modes."[26]

Though Bartók found through folk music a "freedom from the rigid use of the major and minor keys [that] eventually led to a new conception of the chromatic scale, every tone of which came to be considered of equal value and could be used freely and independently," folk music has also been invoked as a means of guaranteeing the opposite result. The notorious February, 1948, Resolution of the Central Committee of the Communist Party on Soviet musical policy saw a failure to "take advantage of the richness of folk melodies, songs, refrains and dance airs, so abundant in the art of the nations of the USSR," as a symptom of "the negation of basic principles of classical music, the preachment of atonality, dissonances and disharmony, supposedly representative of 'progress' and 'modernism' in the development of musical forms; the rejection of such all-important concepts of musical composition as melody, and the infatuation with the confused, neuropathological combinations which transform music into cacophony, into a chaotic agglomeration of sounds"—music "strongly reminiscent of the spirit of contemporary modernistic

[26]Elliott Antokoletz, *The Music of Béla Bartók: A Study of Tonality and Progression in Twentieth-Century Music* (Berkeley and Los Angeles: University of California Press, 1984).

bourgeois music of Europe and America, reflecting the dissolution of bourgeois culture, a complete negation of musical art, its impasse."[27] The "Declaration of the Second International Congress of Composers and Musicologists," meeting in Prague a few months later, "urges composers of the whole world to write music in which high artistic qualities combine with creative individuality and deep and genuine folk art."[28]

Who would deny "how very central music is to our understanding of ourselves"? Must we therefore also accept the conclusions drawn from this premise in a recent book on music as a social art: "Music passes from the separate sphere of the marginal-if-beautiful into the realities of the social world. If music thereby loses its aura, it is granted both the powers and responsibilities of a genuinely political medium."[29] But if music is a "genuinely political medium," it must have a political message. What is that message? Can music that exploits folk elements in a way that led Bartók "to a new conception of the chromatic scale" properly fulfill its political "responsibilities"? Or is this only possible where an affiliation with folk song has the opposite implication, where it acts as an immunizing agent against the tendencies proscribed in the 1948 Resolution of the CCCP, "atonality, dissonances and disharmony"? Can "the powers and responsibilities of a genuinely political medium" as manifested in the music of the past have any relevance for our time? Whatever political meaning the *Eroica Symphony* may have had for Beethoven and may have for us stands utterly opposed to that which the Nazis were able to find in this same work and which enabled them to exploit it for their own

[27]Nicolas Slonimsky, *Music since 1900*, 4th ed., rev. (New York: Charles Scribner's Sons, 1971), pp. 1359f.
[28]Ibid., p. 1379.
[29]Richard Leppert and Susan McClary, eds., *Music and Society: The Politics of Composition, Performance and Reception* (Cambridge, England: Cambridge University Press, 1987), p. xix.

political purposes. It has been suggested that "without words or strong folk elements, it is doubtful if music can convey a clear epic meaning."[30] *Die Meistersinger* has both, but this did not prevent the Nazis from politically exploiting the work in ways that were totally at odds with what the American critic, Paul Rosenfeld, saw as its inherent content. He was revolted by "the image of an audience of Nazi porkers self-righteously taking in the concluding scene of the music drama, identifying their sinister Fascist state with the bright democratic order figured there, adopting the composer as their prophet and justifying their ways to men with his vision."[31]

How can a single work impart such totally different political messages and serve such totally different political purposes? There is, however, no ambiguity at all about what it means to "grant" to music "the powers and responsibilities of a genuinely political medium." To deprive music of its private and personal meaning for us would be to deprive *us* of privacy and personality, and there is no ambiguity about the political meaning of this—there is no ambiguity about the spiritual deprivation that permits a composer to say, in response to the Central Committee's Resolution, "How could it have happened that I failed to introduce a single folk song in the score of my opera? It seems strange and almost incredible to me, and can be explained only as a manifestation of my inherent snobbishness" (Muradeli). Or, "the absence, in my works, of the interpretation of folk art, that great spirit by which our people lives, has been with utmost clarity and definiteness pointed out by the Central Committee. . . . I am deeply grateful for it" (Shostakovich). Or "I must admit that I, too, have

[30]Henry Leland Clarke, "The Basis of Musical Communication," *Journal of Aesthetics and Art History* X/3 (March 1952): 244.
[31]Paul Rosenfeld, "The Nazis and *Die Meistersinger*," in *Musical Impressions: Selections from Paul Rosenfeld's Criticism*, ed. Herbert A. Leibowitz (London: George Allen and Unwin, 1969), p. 18.

indulged in atonality. . . . In the future I hope to get rid of this mannerism" (Prokofiev).[32]

Whatever the political, social, or personal role we may see for music today, there seems to be no shortage in the production of an ample quantity of every kind of music to fill that role, and it is only those who would "grant" to music "the powers and responsibilities of a genuinely political medium" who will want to censor any of it. Even so, this extraordinary proliferation of musical activity, and of musical institutions to promote every aspect and the full range of that activity, is not necessarily a measure of the vitality of our musical culture. A generation of internationally famous figures, many of whom had made contributions to the standard repertory that were familiar to the regular concert-goer in their own time, have passed away, and no similarly acknowledged figures have come along to take their place. But perhaps we don't need any more Stravinskys and Schoenbergs? Pierre Boulez has answered this question in respect to the latter in an address on the occasion of the official opening of the Arnold Schoenberg Institute:

> As some of you may know, I am personally involved very deeply in establishing in Paris a different kind of institute which, at least until now, does not bear the name of a composer but rather describes an intention. We—that is, myself and a team of composers, technicians, and scientists—are in the process of building a research institute founded on the belief that many problems, even the most trivial of them, might be solved by the effort not of a single individual but rather of a whole group. Just as the work of Schoenberg, based on his own technique and on the expansion of his musical thought in unexpected directions, enabled other composers to derive therefrom their own thinking and their own technique, so, in

[32]Slonimsky, *Music since 1900*, pp. 1370, 1371, 1373f.

the same way, a team of investigators, not at all restricted to a limited number of individuals, might help to solve some of the problems which, through either economic pressure or cultural restrictions, have proved very difficult if not insoluble in our musical society at this time.[33]

Though I would not deny the useful work of IRCAM, these words project a concept of cultural progress that is wonderfully consistent with the portrait of life in the last years of the Austro-Hungarian Empire that Robert Musil paints in his novel, *The Man Without Qualities*: "In a community with energies constantly flowing through it, every road leads to a good goal, if one does not spend too much time hesitating and thinking it over. The targets are set up at a short distance, but life is short too, and in this way one gets a maximum of achievement out of it. And man needs no more for his happiness; for what one achieves is what moulds the spirit, whereas what one wants, without fulfilment, only warps it. So far as happiness is concerned it matters very little what one wants; the main thing is that one should get it. Besides, zoology makes it clear that a sum of reduced individuals may very well form a totality of genius."[34]

However, I read the future of music, not in terms of politics or social questions, but only in terms of the self-contained evolution of the musical language. The extraordinary possibilities in a new musical language give me confidence in and hope for the future of music, and though there is no basis at all in logic and history for such an extrapolation from my private and personal experience as a composer, I can't help but persist in the expectation that the social and political future will not make that musical future impossible.

[33]Pierre Boulez, "Through Schoenberg to the Future," *Journal of the Arnold Schoenberg Institute* I/3 (June 1977): 123.

[34]Robert Musil, *The Man Without Qualities*, trans. Eithne Wilkins and Ernst Kaiser (New York: Coward-McCann, 1953), p. 30.

Designer:	Janet Wood
Compositor:	(text) Wilsted & Taylor; (music) Dennis Riley
Text:	11/16 Bembo
Display:	Bembo
Printer:	Edwards Brothers
Binder:	Edwards Brothers

DENSITY 21.5*

Flute Solo

EDGARD VARÈSE

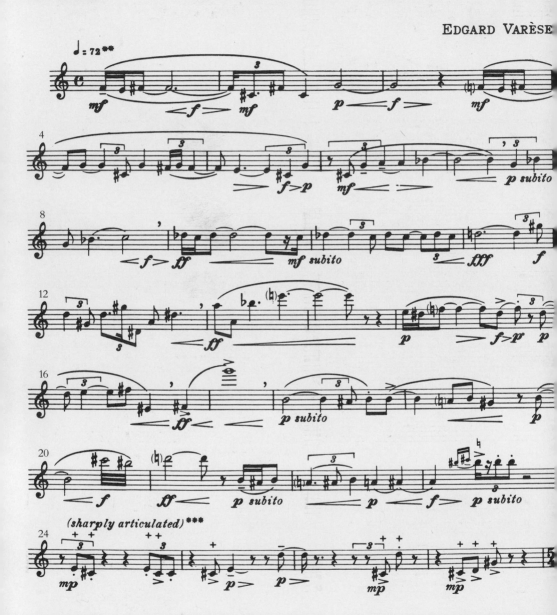

* Written in January, 1936, at the request of Georges Barrère for the inauguration of his platinum flute. Revised April, 1946. 21.5 is the density of platinum.

** Always strictly in time—follow metronomic indications.

*** Notes marked + to be played softly, hitting the keys at the same time to produce a percussive effect.